STARTING WITH SPIRIT

STARTING WITH SPIRIT

Nurturing Your Call
to Pastoral Leadership

Bruce G. Epperly

 ALBAN

Herndon, Virginia
WWW.ALBAN.ORG

The Alban Institute
2121 Cooperative Way, Suite 100
Herndon, VA 20171

Unless otherwise noted, all Scripture quotations are from the New Revised Standard Version of the Bible, © 1989, Division of Christian Education of the National Council of Churches of Christ in the United States of America, and are used by permission.

Cover design by Signal Hill.

Library of Congress Cataloging-in-Publication Data

Epperly, Bruce Gordon.
  Starting with spirit : nurturing your call to pastoral leadership / Bruce G. Epperly.
    p. cm.
  Includes bibliographical references (p. 221).
  ISBN 978-1-56699-408-8
  1. Pastoral theology. 2. Christian leadership. I. Title.
  BV4011.3.E66 2010
  253--dc22

                                    2010044567

10   11   12   13   14   VP   5   4   3   2   1

CONTENTS

A WORD OF THANKS
AND BLESSING

This book reflects seven years of conferences, mentoring, small groups, and chance encounters with newly ordained pastors serving in their first congregational call. I am amazed at their commitment, faithfulness, and perseverance in challenging situations. I am grateful for their willingness to share their stories with me, some anonymously, others publicly. A few of the stories are composites of dozens of conversations I have had with pastors across the country. I have received their permission to tell their stories as a way of paying it forward to the next generation of pastors. I am also grateful to pastors throughout North America who welcomed me into their lives, sharing their ministerial experiences over coffee, lunch, e-mail, and telephone.

I am grateful to the Lilly Endowment, under the direction of Craig Dykstra and John Wimmer, for their generous support of Lancaster Theological Seminary's Wholeness in Ministry program. I am also grateful to the Louisville Institute, under the direction of James Lewis, for its support through a pastoral leadership grant.

Former President Riess Potterveld and Dean Edwin Apon-
te from Lancaster Theological Seminary have constantly supported my efforts in creating innovative programs for ministers,
laypeople, and congregations. I am grateful to the Continuing
Education staff for its faithful excellence in ministering to the
broader community with grace and hospitality. Kathy Harvey
Nelson, April Anderson, and Brenda Marin are colleagues
whose work makes every program and effort world class! They
have made hospitality an art form for our program participants
and leaders. In the course of writing this text, I gratefully received solid research assistance from Brenda Marin and Michelle Owens.

Richard Bass and Beth Gaede of the Alban Institute provided guidance, counsel, support, and suggestions in their
quest to make this book an enduring resource for new pastors.
Andrea Lee provided numerous helpful suggestions.

I cannot conclude this text without giving thanks for my
father, Everett Lewis Epperly (1910–2003), a faithful pastor of
the "old school," who served God with heart, mind, and soul in
congregational and institutional ministry. I also give thanks for
my mother, Loretta Baxter Epperly (1918–1990), whose faith
and personal initiative sustained our family in difficult times.
In 2009 Kate Epperly and I celebrated thirty years of marriage
and also thirty years of ministry. Our marriage and ministry
together has been a holy adventure. Every page has Kate's name
written on it—as my lifelong companion, partner in ministry,
fellow teacher, and great love.

STARTING WITH SPIRIT

I am confident of this, that the one who began a good work among you will bring it to completion by the day of Jesus Christ. . . . And this is my prayer, that your love may overflow more and more with knowledge and full insight to help you determine what is best, so that in the day of Christ, you may be pure and blameless, having produced the harvest of righteousness that comes through Jesus Christ for the glory and praise of God.

— PHILIPPIANS 1:6, 9–11

WHEN I WAS A CHILD, MY AUNT BEULAH AKES TOLD ME A story from my father's childhood. When my father was five years old, she observed him preaching sermons to the chickens in the barnyard of their Iowa family farm. While my dad didn't enter the ordained ministry until thirty years later, his whole life was oriented toward serving the one who called him from his childhood to share good news in small town churches in California and later at a substance abuse center. For more than forty years, my dad dedicated his life to preaching, teaching, and counseling and to accompanying people in their journeys from birth to death. Even after he retired from active ministry, Dad visited people in nursing homes and wrote letters to homebound mem-

1

bers of Grace Baptist Church in San Jose, California, where he worshiped following his retirement from "paid" ministry. He was truly a man of God, to use the archaic language of his generation, whose life found its meaning in sharing the faith he affirmed with heart, mind, and hands. My father was, first and foremost, a pastor.

As a young adult, I vowed never to become a pastor. My dad worked long hours at low pay in small town churches. Although these churches had small memberships, they often made great demands on their pastors in theological orthodoxy, pastoral care, and civic leadership. At one point in his career, he was the subject of controversy and resigned under fire, leaving our family briefly impoverished and the recipient of food baskets and the kindness of strangers. He had deep pastoral relationships that involved hours away from home, and emergency home and hospital visits that interrupted meals, vacations, and Little League games. My mother, Loretta, a traditional minister's wife for most of my childhood, resented these interruptions as well as the intimacy of pastoral relationships that often left my father emotionally drained when he returned home from hospital calls or counseling bereaved people.

But I also remember reading every morning with my dad before the rest of the family got up. My first paid job involved serving as my father's janitorial assistant, making a quarter a week, emptying trash cans in the education wing of Community Baptist Church in King City, California. Later, when I was a college and graduate student, my dad and I took evening walks in which we talked theology, exploring themes like the nature of God, predestination, the scope of salvation, biblical authority, and the second coming of Jesus. I also remember the generosity of my lifelong Republican father-pastor, who invited migrant workers to live in the parsonage garage, gave shelter in the church to peace marchers, and broke the color barrier by ministering to Hispanic farmworkers long before they unionized under Cesar Chavez's leadership. I learned from my father both the joys and the sorrows of faithful ministry as well as the importance of practical theology in shaping people's lives. Even when I left the church during high school and college, the quest for God that was vital to my father's life was also at the heart of my life. That quest took me on an adventure through Buddhist meditation, Hindu philosophy and yoga, and American transcendentalism. Eventually, I became a philosophy and religion major in college and set my sights in graduate school on teaching religion and theology at the college level.

Despite my vow never to enter ordained ministry, I was in many ways my father's son. I experienced the call to ordained ministry midway through my PhD studies at Claremont Graduate University. My future wife, Kate, and I were beginning to get serious about our relationship. Kate was a Disciples of Christ pastor who had returned to Claremont School of Theology to complete her Doctor of Ministry thesis, after a rocky start as an associate minister in a big-steeple congregation in Orange County, California. One morning, as I walked through the lemon orchards near my home in Upland, California, I experienced an intellectual stirring, a gentle whisper, that set me on another pathway: "Give something back to the church that nurtured you." The church that nurtured me as a young adult and toward which I was called in ministry was the mainstream and progressive wing of Christianity, struggling and under siege even in the 1970s. This was the church that enabled me to integrate my high school and college Hindu and Buddhist meditative practices and countercultural inclinations with a vision of God that was inclusive, personally transforming, and socially concerned. In that moment in the lemon grove and in the weeks ahead, I felt a gentle but persistent and growing urge to join body, mind, and spirit—the classroom and the pulpit, the library and the hospital room, the computer and the prophetic word—in service to the faith of Jesus and the good news of God's creative transformation. I felt called to be a teaching pastor, committed to making theology come alive in life-transforming ways in preaching, adult education, and pastoral care.

For more than thirty years, I have followed the call of the Spirit moving through my vocation as a congregational pastor, university chaplain, seminary and university professor, and seminary administrator. The Spirit's movements in my life have led me to some unlikely places and uncomfortable situations. But, following God's Spirit has also given me the opportunity to practice what I teach as well as teach what I practice. Like the prophet Jeremiah, I have come to realize that God was calling me, as God calls everyone in one way or another from infancy, and that at every step of the way, God was luring me forward through insights, inspirations, synchronous encounters, professional experiences, mentors, and the joys of family life and friendship.

God is still calling me to new possibilities for creative ministry and teaching. As I ponder my own ministerial adventure and look forward to the journey that lies ahead, I claim with the apostle Paul, "I am confident of this, that the one who began a good work among you will bring it to completion by the day of Jesus Christ" (Phil. 1:6). I also make that claim for you, whether you are a seminarian, pastor, layperson, or pastor's spouse or partner: I believe that God is working in your life, vocation, and relationships and that God will bring God's good work in your life to fullness. The Spirit that gave you life and breath continues to inspire your journey of faith and ministry moment by moment and day by day.

Writing this book has emerged from my pastoral adventure of joining academic reflection and pastoral ministry. For the past several years, I have experienced God's call in my work with pastors involved in Lancaster Theological Seminary's programs for ministers in every season of life.[1] I have experienced the whispers of the Spirit, often coming to me in "sighs too deep for words" (Rom. 8:26), echoing in the voices of nearly a hundred new pastors in the seminary's Wholeness in Ministry program. All of them in one way or another have confessed, "I know God has called me to ministry, but the task seems too great and my talents too meager. How can I find ways to be faithful amid the challenges of ministry? How can I be a good pastor and yet have quality time with my kids and spouse?" My vocation at this point of my life is many faceted, but I experience the call to integrate seminary and congregational transformation by helping new pastors continue to grow in their experience of the call of the Spirit as they take their first steps in the adventure of ordained ministry.

This book is about *starting with spirit* in the transition from seminary to congregational leadership. God's Spirit calls people to ordained ministry and provides guidance to pastors every step of the way. We pastors simply need to pause long enough to experience the ubiquitous movements of the Spirit in our lives. We need to develop habits and practices that keep us in touch with God in the mundane as well as the dramatic moments of ministry. This text invites new pastors, and pastors in every season of ministry, to nurture the call they received once upon a time in ways that deepen their spiritual lives, nurture faithful excellence and effectiveness in ministry, bring joy to their families and friends, and give glory to the one who inspires their pastoral journeys.

I believe that ministry can be a joyful and life transforming for pastors as well as their congregants and families. Wholeness and effectiveness in ministry is not accidental but the result of a commitment to deepen the initial experience of call through continuing education, spiritual practices, healthy relationships, and creative responses to transition and conflict.

The Perils and Promises of Ministry

As you reflect on your ministry today, whether you are just beginning or have been an ordained minister for decades, take a moment to reflect on these words from United Church of Christ pastor Lillian Daniel: "I love being a minister. Even when ministry is hard, it is more fun than any job I can imagine.

Where else can you preach, teach, meet with a lead abatement specialist, and get arrested for civil disobedience all in the same week? Where else can you be invited into the living rooms of new mothers and into the hospice rooms of the dying, and find hope in both places? ... But mostly I love observing God's presence in the lives of people of faith."[2]

Not all pastors are as sanguine about their vocation as Lillian Daniel. Listen to the confession of noted preacher and author Barbara Brown Taylor: "I had once again become so busy caring for the household of God that I had neglected the One who called me there. If I still had plenty of energy for the work, that was because feeding others was still my food. As long as I fed them, I did not feel my hunger pains. . . . The demands of parish ministry routinely cut me off from the resources I needed to do parish ministry. I knew where God's fire was burning, but I could not get to it."[3]

Which of these descriptions of ministry do you identify with as you consider your own current well-being and joy in ministry? Is your heart filled with joy as you begin a new week of ministry? Or does Monday morning bring a weariness of the spirit and depression at another week of sermon writing, visitation, and congregational business? Or are you somewhere in-between, inspired by the vision of healthy and joyful ministry but constantly caught up in the details of your pastoral week and only occasionally experiencing a sense of God's presence and inspiration?

Inspired by my work with nearly one hundred pastors in Lancaster Theological Seminary's Wholeness in Ministry program as well as conversations and workshops with newly ordained pastors across the United States and Canada, this book is intended to be a spiritual and professional resource for new pastors, their family members, and congregations as well as ministers in every season of ministry as they seek to grow in vitality and skill in the ongoing adventure of ministry.

Throughout this text, I will be sharing stories and insights from pastors across North America as well as providing creative and life-sustaining guidance for people taking their first steps in congregational ministry.

Congregational ministry is a challenge today, but I believe that pastors can be healthy, effective, and inspired throughout their professional lives. In the early 1990s, I began teaching courses in professional well-being at Georgetown University's law and medical schools. A pivotal question I asked program participants was, "Will you be glad that you entered this profession twenty years from now? Will your spouse, partner, children, and other intimate companions also feel grateful that you entered this profession twenty years from now?" I address this same spiritual examination of conscience to new pastors today. If you are a new pastor, consider the following questions: Fresh from seminary graduation and beginning your first congregational call, will you experience joy in ministry today? Twenty years from now, will you and those who love you be glad you accepted the call to ordained ministry? Will you have the creativity and courage to respond to unanticipated challenges in culture and congregational life? My prayer is that your answer will always be yes, especially at those times when ministry is difficult and complex.

When pastors start with spirit—that is, begin their ministries with a commitment both to faithful excellence as pastors and to well-being of body, mind, spirit, and relationships—they will experience a sense of joy and meaning amid the challenges of ministry. Healthy and effective ministry is the result of the interplay of intentionality and grace. The one who called us to ordained ministry and spiritual leadership always provides the inspiration and energy we need to be faithful in our calling. But God's call invites our response, our willingness to say yes to wholeness and growth in ministry for the glory of God and the healing of the earth.

Vision, Promise, and Practice

Starting with spirit in ministry is a profoundly theological and spiritual task.[4] Our theology of ministry and understanding of God's presence in the world shape how we live out our ministerial vocation, especially in times of transition and novelty. While there are many possible theologies and practices of ministry, I believe that the apostle Paul's letter to the Philippians provides a solid theological road map for new pastors who are crossing the boundary from seminary to their first congregational call. Without a vision or life-supporting theology, both pastors and congregations will find themselves without a compass in the holy adventure of ministry. Paul begins with an affirmation and promise: "The one who began a good work among you will bring it to completion by the day of Jesus Christ" (Phil. 1:6). Faithful excellence in ministry finds its inspiration in the recognition that God is constantly and persistently working in our lives, seeking our personal and vocational wholeness and excellence. Jesus's promise, "I came that they may have life, and have it abundantly" (John 10:10), is an ongoing reminder that in every moment and encounter, God is providing you with all the resources and energy you will need for faithful excellence in ministry. Your call to ministry is part of a much larger divine call, embracing all creation, that began at your conception and will lure you forward on a holy adventure all the days of your life. Ministry that transforms, refreshes, and inspires begins by affirming God's omnipresence and loving guidance in our lives. You are not alone in your ministry. God is your caring and challenging companion every step of the way.

The call to ministry is constantly growing and evolving in each pastor's life. When we answer the call to ordained ministry, we begin a journey that will take us to unexpected places and call us to expand our personal and professional boundaries. Just as Jesus challenged Peter to fish in deeper waters, God calls pastors to explore new ways of ministry and constantly open ourselves to new ideas and practices in ministerial leadership. In the spirit of philosopher Alfred North Whitehead's words, new pastors are called to creatively originate novelty to match the novelties of their environment. For that reason, in the transition from seminary to congregational leadership, new pastors must be willing to see the world with new eyes and respond to the congregation in new and creative ways. They are called from their first days in seminary to nurture what Craig Dykstra, vice president for religion at Lilly Foundation, has called "the pastoral imagination," a way of interpreting life that shapes everything a pastor experiences and does so that he or she might fully claim the vocation of pastor.[5] As a thirtysomething Disciples of Christ pastor confessed, "For the first few months at my new congregation, when someone called out 'pastor,' I often looked around to see where the pastor was. Now, I know that I am a pastor and I claim my new calling every day. I *am* a pastor." A Presbyterian pastor adds: "I have discovered that being a pastor is a way of life. I can't turn it off at five o'clock. It shapes how I respond to situations not only at church, but in the shopping center and at home. While I don't try to be the pastor to my husband and kids, I know that my integrity as a pastor depends of treating them with the same care and patience as I treat my congregants, and vice versa. More than ever, I know that I must practice what I preach at home as well as at church."

Paul's words to the Philippians contain a life-transforming promise for new pastors: I am confident that the one who began a good work among you will bring it to fulfillment. They also provide practical guidance for claiming your role as God's partner in your own personal and professional growth and in the vocation of pastoral leadership. Healthy and effective ministry throughout one's professional life is also inspired by a spirit of hopefulness and trust in God's ongoing creativity and inspiration amid the small and large challenges of ministry.

Starting with spirit in ministry is a dynamic process of call and response. God is constantly calling, and our responses to

God shape God's next movements in our lives. When we abide in Christ's life-giving presence, we will bear much fruit in our ministry and relationships (John 15:1–11). And so it follows that life-transforming ministry joins grace and intentionality. Paul captures the lively interplay of call and response in his counsel to "work out your own salvation with fear and trembling; for it is God who is at work in you, enabling you both to will and to work for his good pleasure" (Phil. 2:12–13).

Ministry is holy and challenging work, and the health of the church and the well-being of congregants depend on the pastor's character, commitment, and professionalism. But through the dangers, toils, and snares of ordained ministry, we must never forget that we are never alone; God's amazing grace is working within us and within those we serve to bring God's vision into reality in individual and community life.

God's promises of wholeness and fulfillment in ministry are intended to inspire us to ministerial excellence. While no one size fits all, and spiritual practices transform us most when they reflect our unique personality, age, life setting, and congregational context, the apostle Paul provides the Philippians and us with practices that lead to faithful excellence and well-being for pastors in their first congregational call: "Finally, beloved, whatever is true, whatever is honorable, whatever is just, whatever is pure, whatever is pleasing, whatever is commendable, if there is any excellence and if there is anything worthy of praise, think about these things. Keep on doing the things that you have learned and received and heard and seen in me, and the God of peace will be with you" (Phil. 4:8–9).

The ongoing nurture of the pastoral imagination involves cultivating specific vocational practices and ways of interpreting life events. God is with us, constantly inviting us to serve as Christ's companions and representatives in the world through ministries of word, sacrament, presence, and prophetic challenge. When we, through faithfully committing ourselves to spiritual practices and professional formation, holistically embody the call we received, we grow in pastoral imagination and faithful excellence in ministry. As the Benedictine spiritual tradition affirms, life-transforming ministry involves seeing Christ in every face and awakening other people to God's presence in their lives and social settings. This interplay of theological vision and spiritual and professional practice enables pastors to grow in the call to ministry that initially inspired us to enroll in seminary and accept our first congregational call. Starting with spirit in the journey from seminary to our first congregational call grafts our ministry in the ever-nourishing vine of Christ, which enables our ministry to grow, blossom, and bear much fruit, whether the soil is rich or rocky.

CHAPTER I

OPENING THE DOOR

Now the word of the LORD came to me saying, "Before I
formed you in the womb I knew you, and before you were
born I consecrated you; I appointed you a prophet to the
nations." Then I said, "Ah, Lord GOD! Truly I do not know
how to speak, for I am only a boy." But the LORD said to
me, "Do not say, 'I am only a boy'; for you shall go to all to
whom I send you, and you shall speak whatever I command
you. Do not be afraid of them, for I am with you to deliver
you, says the LORD."

—JEREMIAH 1:4–8

WHILE FEW NEW SEMINARY GRADUATES DIRECTLY HEAR
the voice of God as they begin their first pastorate, most new
pastors can identify with Jeremiah's feelings of inadequacy and
ill-preparedness. They have left the security of seminary classes
and field education settings to pastor on their own without a
safety net. Most newly ordained ministers feel a combination
of grief and anticipation as they begin their first days as congregational leaders. In this chapter, I will focus on the first few
months of a pastor's transition from seminary life to congregational leadership by relating the stories of new pastors' first
experiences, challenges, and best practices in this time of new
beginnings for both the pastor and her or his congregation.

First Impressions

Lutheran pastor and Duke professor Richard Lischer describes his ambivalence upon driving by the church where he would soon serve. "I felt something flop in my stomach. Then, a crushing sense of disappointment. *So this is what has been prepared for me,* I thought, as if something surely *should* have been prepared for me." As he surveyed the grounds, Lischer pondered, "So this is where we [his wife and daughter Sarah] would make our home. What kind of life would it be?"[1]

Joe, a United Church of Christ pastor, felt the same letdown when he moved into the parsonage next door to his town-and-country congregation near Reading, Pennsylvania, a few weeks before he was to begin his ministry. Due to be married the next month, Joe discovered a dirty parsonage and a torn-up basement. He spent the first month of his ministry painting and cleaning to make a home for his new bride.

Phyllis, another United Church of Christ pastor serving in a suburban York, Pennsylvania, congregation remembers, "On the day after my ordination, no one welcomed me at my first congregation. I opened the church doors with a key that the interim minister had given me. To my dismay, I found a study that had been used for a storage room and a dirty desk, piled high with papers." Now, after fourteen successful years at this congregation, Phyllis recalls, "How different the church profile was from the reality I faced that first day!" Tom, an American Baptist pastor in Western Ohio, remembers the same sinking feeling when he discovered not only that the church secretary was inept at both personal relationships and technology but also that he had to share an office with her. He soon realized that if he were to have any privacy at all, he would have to work at home until a new secretary could be found—two years later!

In contrast, Becky, an associate pastor at a United Church of Christ congregation in Hagerstown, Maryland, fell in love with her congregation from her very first encounter. Welcomed by a supportive senior pastor who showed her the ropes and mentored her as she took her first steps in ministry, Becky recalls "how friendly these people were from the very beginning and how supportive they still are of my ministry and my family."

First impressions, those of the new pastor and of the congregation, can make or break a new pastor's ministry. Zen Buddhists speak of encountering the world with the *beginner's mind*, and new pastors need to approach their first congregational call with that same sense of novelty and wonder. In *Tending to the Holy*, Kate Epperly and I reflected on Gerald May's spiritual practice of *pausing, noticing, opening, stretching and yielding*, as the prelude to *responding* and *acting* in any ministerial situation. If our lives are part of God's holy adventure, then even the most ambiguous pastoral situations can be the source of insight and growth for all parties, provided that they look for—and trust—God's presence in every encounter. No congregation entirely reflects the description conveyed by its congregational profile, the search committee's hopes, or the bishop or district superintendant's portrayal. Nor does any flesh-and-blood pastor entirely reflect her or his paper credentials or references. Congregations are, as the apostle Paul notes throughout his letters, flesh-and-blood communities that both embrace and turn away from the gospel mandate.

New pastors are most successful in the transition from seminary to their first congregation when they expect and accept imperfection as an essential ingredient in the art of ministry. While some congregations are clearly dysfunctional and may even fall into the category of "clergy killers," most congregations are healthy enough to provide adequate support, challenge, and acceptance for pastors embarking on their first call.

The Challenges of Inadequacy

Regardless of her or his age, every new pastor, like the young prophet Jeremiah, feels inadequate as he or she faces the calling to be congregational teacher, preacher, and pastor. In his classic description of his first years in ministry, *Leaves from the Notebook of a Tamed Cynic*, theologian Reinhold Niebuhr makes the following confession: "There is something ludicrous about a callow young fool like myself standing up to preach a sermon to these good folks. I talk wisely about life and know little about life's problems. I tell them of the need to sacrifice, although most of them could tell me something about what that really means."[2] Initially unsure about some of his pastoral roles, Niebuhr shares a vignette that many new pastors can relate to as they make their pastoral calls. "Usually I walked past the house two or three times before I summoned the courage to go in."[3]

Joanne remembers her first week as pastor of a United Church of Christ congregation near Allentown, Pennsylvania. That first Monday, when she reported to work, she asked herself, "What do I do now? I had no idea what to do!" Joanne is grateful that her anxious contemplations were interrupted by the stream of visitors who greeted her throughout her first week and through their hospitality helped her to take the first steps in claiming her role as pastor. Karen, the pastor of a Mennonite church near Lancaster, Pennsylvania, recalls feeling the pressure of being the first woman pastor in her congregation's long history. "I believed that if the congregation had a bad experience, this would reflect on all women in the ministry."

Sara, the pastor of a union Evangelical Lutheran in America–United Church of Christ congregation near Reading, Pennsylvania, was surprised at how quickly people came to her with their problems, even though they barely knew her. Although she had worked at the district attorney's office, she was shocked at "the extreme brokenness of people, both those who endured pain in their family lives and those who had been hurt by the church!" Karen echoes Sara's surprise at the level of intimacy she experienced from the very beginning of her ministry: "I experienced a tremendous amount of trust at the beginning. Although I was their first woman pastor in a denomination that is still ambivalent about the ordination of women, they invited me into their lives, trusting my character and ability to hold confidences." Still, as George, a United Methodist pastor in the Washington, D.C., suburbs recalls, "I felt over my head as I confronted the challenges of my first counseling appointment. I felt helpless in responding to the crisis my congregant was facing. But I sat and listened, and despite my inexperience, I prayed. While I wasn't prepared for the issue he brought to me, I believe that God was with us." Two years later, George's congregant is still in the church and has really turned a corner in his life.

Every new pastor experiences the awesome task of speaking about the infinite God, sharing in people's traumas, and being invited into moments of growth and transformation. Few of us feel worthy of the task and are often overwhelmed by trust we receive from people who barely know us. We know that the task requires the grace and guidance of the Creative and Graceful Wisdom beyond ourselves. We also know that we must be worthy of the trust we receive as preachers, teachers, healers, and spiritual guides. This challenges new pastors to seek the guidance of experienced mentors and colleague groups and to take seriously their own spiritual lives and professional growth. Although much of congregational ministry is private and should remain so, no pastor can go it alone. It takes a community of colleagues and spiritual guides to nurture healthy and effective ministry over the long haul.

A Season of Firsts

Ministry is a series of firsts that may initially overwhelm a newly ordained pastor. Echoing Jeremiah, Lischer observes, "My congregants were expected to welcome an inexperienced twenty-eight-year-old stranger into a community as tightly sealed as a jar of canned pickles. The church had decreed that henceforth I would be spiritual guide, public teacher, and

beloved sage with a stroke of a wand. God—or the bishop—
had just made me an expert in troubled marriages, alcoholism,
teen sex, and farm subsidies."[4]

The enormity of the transition from seminary to being a
congregational pastor finally hit Lischer at the service of installation. He listened as the bishop asked the congregation,
"Are you willing to receive your pastor as a minister of God and
show him love, honor, and obedience in the Lord?" As Lischer
recollects, "They said, 'I do' or words to that effect, and the next
thing I knew, we were married."[5]

My most anxious "first" in ministry involved performing my
first wedding. My field education pastor never explained to me
how to plan a wedding or lead a wedding rehearsal. I had only
attended one rehearsal before, and that was for my own wedding! Thankfully, my wife Kate, who was a year ahead of me in
ministerial experience, showed me the ropes. Somehow, I survived the chaos of that first rehearsal with minimal mishaps,
despite a racing heart.

Faced early on in their first call with the death of a congregant, other new pastors discover how quickly a pastor must
move from grief counselor to liturgical organizer and nego-
tiator with the funeral home. Steve, an Evangelical Lutheran
Church in America (ELCA) pastor in Western Maryland, received a telephone call the morning after his first sermon telling
him of a search committee member's sudden death.

> I was shocked by the news and wondered what I was sup-
> posed to do. Seminary didn't spend a lot of time on funer-
> als. I had the book of worship to get me through the service
> but was uncertain how to proceed in responding to the family
> and the funeral home. Thank God, I had a seasoned pastor
> I could call who guided me through the process. After the
> funeral, I went home and slept the rest of the afternoon; my
> first funeral was that stressful!

The firsts of ministry are usually stressful, but they are often joyful too. I still recall the joy of the first time I baptized three babies on an Easter Sunday. A little later I navigated both literally and figuratively my first adult baptisms at a Disciples of Christ congregation, doing my best not to drown the baptizands or go down with them in the barely heated baptistery!

In their first few months of ministry, new pastors journey through a series of firsts in their new role as spiritual leader: first pastoral report, first board meeting, first confirmation class, first controversy, and first hospital visit. This is an adventurous time in which new pastors take the first steps not only in defining their ministry with a new congregation but also in shaping their ministerial practice and theology over the long haul.

Grief and Transitions

Change and transition are at the heart of life. Creative transformation always requires loss. While vocational and geographical transitions are often a source of anticipation and new life, most of us also experience grief when we let go of what has been stable and familiar in our lives to embrace the novelty toward which God calls us. As they begin their first congregational call, new pastors typically experience grief at leaving the friends, intellectual stimulation, and professional safety of seminary life. They also enter congregations that may be grieving the loss of a long-term pastor, diminished membership, a predecessor's pastoral ineffectiveness or misconduct, or changes in the nature of ministry itself. While grief is painful, it may also be a source of growth for congregations and pastors alike when they recognize that they are partners in accepting past losses and awakening to future possibilities.

When Sarah, an Episcopal pastor, opened the door to her parsonage in upstate New York, she was delighted by how well it had been prepared for her arrival. She was eager to move her possessions out of storage and into her new home, but she also felt a deep loneliness.

> I guess you could say I was ambivalent. The parsonage was lovely and had room enough for my friends to comfortably visit. But now I was all alone. At seminary, I lived in a modest apartment, but I could go downstairs anytime to talk theology, commiserate about my field education supervisor, or complain about the glacial pace of finding a call. Now, I had no one to talk with. As a single woman and introvert, I'm attracted to the monastic life, but only in small doses. I wondered with whom I would share the challenges of my first call.

Sarah could have retreated to her parsonage and immersed herself entirely in congregational life, but she reached out. She found another single woman minister in the area, joined a lectionary colleague group, and kept in regular touch with her friends via Facebook and Skype. She also discovered a book group meeting at a local independent bookstore that enabled her to meet people outside the church and the ministry. She met monthly with an experienced woman pastor with whom she shared the challenges of her first call and regularly asked for counsel as she navigated the firsts of this new season in ministry.

Although the profession of ministry is, by nature, public and relational, it is often lonely for single pastors and clergy spouses and partners. While feelings of loneliness and loss profoundly affect single pastors who may not have a partner or intimate friend in the neighborhood with whom to share the joys and challenges of life and ministry, married pastors and their spouses may also feel isolated and alone. They have to come to grips with schedules that are often at cross-purposes. As Sharon, a United Methodist pastor in Eastern Pennsylvania, notes, "My husband often feels abandoned on the weekends. He's ready to go out with me and the kids, when my job requires me to work all day Sunday and often spend Saturdays working on my sermon or at weddings, church bazaars, and hospital visitation." Charlie, who pastors a town-and-country ELCA congregation in Eastern Pennsylvania, speaks for both single and married pastors when he says:

> At seminary I used to love to get together with friends to talk about theology or justice issues. But here, the other pastors are more conservative, and I'm an hour drive from any of my seminary peers. I pastor a loving congregation, but they couldn't care less about postmodern theology, the emerging church, or what Dietrich Bonhoeffer said about the modern situation. I win points with them when I can talk about the Washington Redskins or Baltimore Ravens, or meet with the locals at the greasy spoon for biscuits and gravy. I sure miss the opportunity to talk theology with peers over lunch or a glass of beer.

While we may come to love our congregants, pastors must maintain a professional distance in ministry. While pastors may eat at congregants' homes and spend hours on projects with church members, healthy ministry requires that their closest relationships be outside the church. This arrangement is especially difficult for pastors whose calls have taken them far away from home or seminary. In spite of the excitement most new pastors feel as they begin their first congregational call, the novelty of ministry is bittersweet for those who leave the familiarity of seminary life. Every adventure involves letting go and grieving the loss of familiar friendships and rituals.

Striking the Right Balance in Making Changes in the Church

Often pastors forget that their very entry into a new congregation shakes up congregational life. Even if you preached your predecessor's sermons word for word for several weeks, adopting her or his style and delivery, congregants would experience both the joy and the anxiety that change brings. One new pastor confessed, "Although I felt a bit insecure about what I was to do at first and knew that eventually plenty needed to be done for this church to return to vitality, I began with baby steps." While each of us has her or his own unique style, personality type, and way of responding to new situations, pastoral wisdom suggests that unless a crisis immediately confronts your congregation's ministry, pastors are most effective over the long haul when they begin deliberately, yet purposefully, making changes in the first few months of their first congregational call. To get a sense of the context of your ministry and the places where you can begin to make changes, take time to look over your predecessor's worship services and reports to the church board and get to know the recent history of your congregation, including its most recent successes and setbacks. This will give you a sense of the congregation's and its pastors' approaches to innovation in the past.

When Phyllis was called to be pastor of a midsized suburban congregation in York, Pennsylvania, she wanted to exercise her spiritual and pastoral leadership from the first day. She recalls thinking, "'You've called me, so I can change things now!' I wanted results!" As Phyllis remembers, however, the congregation also wanted changes, "but they didn't want to rock the boat." Phyllis relates one incident in which her desire to make the Sunday school rooms more inviting inadvertently led to hurt feelings in her congregation. After doing a walkthrough of the Sunday school rooms with one of the Christian education committee members, she commented that the rooms needed to be painted and redecorated in order to be welcoming to children and their parents. She discovered much to her chagrin that the classrooms had just been painted and refurbished by the church school team. The classrooms that looked beautiful to them seemed drab and ugly to Phyllis. Now, fourteen years later, Phyllis wishes she had moved more slowly in the first months of her ministry.

In the spirit of Jesus's counsel, effective ministry requires pastors to be "in but not of" their congregations, even if their denominational polity requires membership in the congregation they serve. As pastors, our first loyalty is to God's vision for the congregation and its mission to the wider world. While pastors can never claim to know completely God's call for their ministries and congregations, nevertheless they must filter all congregational encounters through the lens of their pastoral imagination. Most pastors want to get along and be accepted in their communities, but their education, calling, and loyalty to Christ and Christ's church sets them at a creative distance from those to whom they minister. Further, new pastors, especially in mainline denominations, are often more theologically and socially liberal than their congregants. New pastors must learn to strike a balance between standing apart from and fitting in with the congregations they serve. They must also learn to distinguish among issues of integrity, leadership style, and theological perspective. While pastors may eventually seek to guide their congregations toward significant changes in theology, worship, and outreach, many new pastors find it important to follow the maxim "Don't sweat the small stuff," until they gain greater awareness of their community and receive greater authority from their congregants.

Whether they are preaching, providing spiritual leadership, or conducting the business of the church, new pastors need to remember the insights of congregational systems theory. An effective leader must balance self-differentiation with connectedness; her or his call to transformation must be spoken in ways that address the congregation's particular culture and decision-making process. She must claim pastoral authority, and this means articulating a clear vision of the church and the gospel mandate as she understands it, but this vision needs to be articulated in ways that affirm and embrace rather than demean and alienate those who take different approaches to faith and ethics. The old adage "Preach the gospel and love the people" still works in pastoral ministry. "Preach the gospel" means being faithful to God's vision above all else, and it may mean that on some issues the pastor may choose to be the minority voice in the congregation. "Love the people" means that in the way we both share our vision and stand apart from our congregants, we intend to inspire others to listen, reflect, and join us on a journey in faithful service to Christ. Seeing with the eyes of Christ, we may discover that even the most recalcitrant congregant is also God's beloved son or daughter.

Intimacy and Distance in Pastoral Relationships

New pastors and congregations are typically ambivalent about how they should relate to one another, especially in the first months of ministry. On the one hand, a new pastor is an outsider who is called to spiritual leadership. Her vocation, education, and expertise differentiate her from most of her congregants. She is called to speak for God and to place the well-being of her congregants and the church above friendship and popularity. While congregants often want their pastors to mirror them theologically and politically, healthy congregants know that a good pastor must stand apart precisely because of his vocation as teacher, minister, and pastor. In the same way that people allow physicians physical intimacy as a result of their doctor's expertise and professional code of ethics, congregants give pastors immediate spiritual intimacy in hospital rooms and counseling sessions, because they know that their pastor's education, professional ethics, spiritual formation, and vocation set him or her apart for a unique role. On the other hand, new pastors want to be liked, and often parishioners want to be the pastor's new best friend. As a result, pastors and congregants share in a constantly shifting dance of intimacy and distance, which reflects Jesus's own relationship to his first followers. Jesus could challenge Peter because Peter knew that Jesus loved him, and Peter could take Jesus's challenge to heart because both Peter and Jesus both knew that their intimacy did not compromise Jesus's vocational authority.

This quest to balance relationship and professionalism appropriate to the pastoral vocation can lead to both challenging and humorous encounters. Richard Lischer tells the story of being invited to join a group of older men one afternoon in the basement den of a congregant's home. After a few minutes of conversation, Bertie, the host, "fixed me," as Lischer recalls, "with his cagey blue eyes and asked offhandedly, 'Pastor, will you have a beer?'" All eyes were trained on the pastor as he responded, "Sure." Lischer enjoyed his Budweiser until he noticed that he was the only one drinking. When he asked if his host was having one, he replied that he wasn't imbibing "in a tone that seemed to ask, 'What kind of man would drink beer at two in the afternoon?'" Recalling that moment in his first pastorate, Lischer asks, "The point of the exercise? The new pastor is either one of the boys or a moral slacker. I left unsure of my grade."[6]

Joe experienced this same dissonance when he found himself at a social gathering where alcohol was being served. After considering the matter for a moment, Joe decided to "be who I am and to have a glass of wine." Later that evening, Joe wondered, "Did I do the right thing?" In the more accepting environment of seminary, the question "To drink or not to drink?" was a nonissue, yet such concerns can take on paramount importance in a pastor's first congregational call.

Some pastors, fresh from boundary training, clearly and decisively rebuff congregants' attempts at friendship. Susan remembers the hurt look on a congregant's face when in response to her comment, "I'm so glad that we're friends," Susan asserted, "I'm your pastor, I can't be your friend." "Immediately, I wished I could take that comment back. I could have been a bit more nuanced in affirming my pastoral relationship with her. Although we eventually had a close working relationship, I hurt her feelings and made her feel foolish by my bluntness."

I am a firm advocate of pastors articulating good but flexible boundaries related to their work schedule, need for privacy, professional role, and physical and emotional intimacy. Nevertheless, new pastors need to discover creative ways to respond to their congregants' desire for friendship. Their congregants want the pastor to like them, too. Since most congregants have no experience in family systems theory or boundary training, they may assume that outside the pulpit, the pastor is just like anyone else and can be a partner in bowling, shopping, sporting events, gossip, and emotional intimacy. A good sense of boundaries undergirds faithful excellence in ministry; yet, an inflexible approach to congregants often leads to alienation and mistrust on the part of congregants. Jesus loved his followers, and we are called to love our congregants, but this love takes place within the crucible of healthy professional relationships. While each pastor will respond differently to overtures of friendship, Susan notes that today her response would have been, "I like you, too. But you have to remember that, first of all, I'm your pastor, and that's at the heart of our relationship."

New pastors often need to check with mentors or colleague groups about appropriate pastoral distance. Virtually every pastor has *dual roles* in his congregation. For example, a teenager in the youth group may babysit for the pastor's five-year-old when he is at a meeting or going out for dinner. Congregants may bring fruit and vegetables to the single pastor or the pastor and her family. The pastor may be invited as a nonpaying guest to a congregant's club, go bowling or golfing with a congregant and have a drink in the bar afterwards, or receive an invitation to use a parishioner's cabin for his vacation. All of these encounters, if handled prayerfully and carefully, solidify a pastor's relationships with the congregation and enable her or him to be welcomed in moments of crisis and challenge. Still, the dance of pastoral relatedness goes on, and new pastors need to regularly reflect on their pastoral relationships and adjust their behavior in order to find a proper balance of intimacy and professional distance. In the end, we as pastors cannot control or dictate how congregants respond to us, but we can be aware of our own motivations and uphold the highest standards of personal and professional ethics.

Sometimes pastors need to differentiate themselves culturally or ethically from their congregants to be faithful to the gospel as they understand it. Although Mark was more conservative than most of his seminary classmates, this United Methodist pastor soon discovered that he was among the most liberal members of his Western Pennsylvania congregation. Evangelical in theology, a hunter by hobby, and Republican by party, Mark nevertheless recognized and appreciated diversity in theological positions, ethnicity, sexual orientation, and politics. He didn't know quite what to say when one of his parishioners ranted, "President Obama is a socialist, a Muslim, and not even an American citizen." At first, he simply said nothing but wondered if, as a pastor, he had an obligation to challenge falsehoods and racial epithets uttered by members of his congregation. He was put to the test when on a hunting trip a few of his congregants began to make more insidious racist comments about President Obama and Muslims.

> I could see that some in the group were becoming uneasy with the way the conversation was going. I began to feel anxious and wondered if I should say something. If I kept silent, they would assume I agreed with their racist comments or lacked the moral courage to confront them. I finally decided to take a stand. I prefaced my words by saying, "Well, you know I'm not President Obama's biggest fan, but I wonder what Jesus would say about him. After all, Obama's a Christian, too, and the Bible says we should pray for our leaders." After a moment of silence, everyone went back to hunting, but as mild as my comments were, I think I made the point that I as their pastor had limits, and I wouldn't stand for racist comments in our church.

While some of us might have more forcefully challenged these racist comments than Mark, we have to remember that location is everything in ministry, and that location includes both our own and our congregants' political and theological perspectives. Encouraging new ways of thinking in a congregation is often a step-by-step process of challenging old prejudices and exploring new ways of thinking, rather than rushing to condemnation and judging ideologies that seem foreign to the pastor's understanding of Christianity.

The Pastor as Detective

A good pastor needs to join appropriate boundaries with curiosity about the human condition. In *Tending to the Holy*, Kate Epperly and I noted that, in the spirit of North African monastics, the pastor should be "all eye" and "all sense" as she observes the physical, spiritual, and emotional environment that surrounds her. This curiosity and awareness is essential for good ministry as well.

One of my favorite detective shows is *Colombo*. In that series, the cagey Colombo appears to be clueless as he fumbles his way through murder investigations. He solves cases, so it appears, only by accident and good luck. While pastors may not wish to be viewed by their congregants as the dumbest person in the room, pastors as observers, spiritual ethnographers, and keepers of secrets always know more than they can tell. To keep confidentiality and promote healing within the congregation, pastors often have to play dumb in situations in which they know more than they can let on.

New pastors enter a multidimensional, nuanced, and confusing world when they begin their first call. Things are not always as they seem. Pastors may intuit certain unspoken communal understandings, past experiences of misconduct and betrayal, feuds and alliances, and secrets that "everybody knows about." Successful pastors take time to listen well to the spoken and unspoken messages of their congregants in order to discern how best to minister. Observation enables pastors not only to be healers but also to avoid issues of triangulation and unintentional offense. Careful observation also forces pastors to listen before they speak and to speak to the real, rather than assumed, situations in their congregation's life.

A pastor's spiritual detective work may begin by going over documents such as board minutes, congregational histories, and financial records. Phyllis notes, "I had to get access to certain things in order to respond to what I perceived were unspoken issues in the church. I made it a point to study the financial records in order to assess accurately the congregation's financial situation." In response to missteps in her first congregational call, Lois now begins new ministerial assignments with the question, "What are they used to in worship, and who selects the hymns?" before making significant changes in the congregation's worship service. Attentiveness to the congregation's style of worship avoids confusion and controversy in a new pastor's first few months in a new congregation.

Every detective, from Sherlock Holmes to Miss Marple, knows that things are not always what they seem. One pastor recalls the sage advice she received from a more experienced colleague: "Be careful of the people who greet you most warmly at first. It may not be friendship they're after, but gaining your support for their cause." This same pastor noted that beneath the kind words of some of her earliest visitors was an agenda about how worship should be conducted, who should be dismissed from teaching Sunday school, or how many hours the pastor should spend in her office. On the other hand, as Becky, an associate pastor in Hagerstown, Maryland, notes, the support of congregants from the first moments of ministry may reflect authentic care rather than a hidden agenda: "What I experienced at the beginning has persisted through my ministry of nearly five years. The people welcomed me with open arms from the very beginning and have supported me all through my ministry, including my pregnancy and parenting of a young child."

Being a congregational detective is a spiritual practice. It involves listening with the heart as well as the ears. As Christian leaders, we need to affirm the presence of God, often expressed in sighs too deep for words, in the most challenging of congregants. And so as pastors we look for something *more* in each person we meet, perhaps a deeper longing for God, the need to be loved, an abusive experience that has shaped her or his life, or hidden anger or low self-esteem. We must be wise as serpents yet gentle as doves as we tend to the holy in ministry.

As spiritual ethnographers, we train our ears to hear congregants' experiences of God as well as their experiences of our new congregation. We listen for what gives them joy, the meanings they attribute to worship and congregational programs, and their concept of ministry. While our listening does not imply agreement and may not change our approach to worship or pastoral leadership, deep spiritual listening helps new pastors appropriately respond to individuals as well as the congregational system itself.

How we open the door in a new congregation is crucial. While ministry includes much that we cannot control, faithful and effective ministry is grounded in flexible intentionality, self-awareness, healthy boundaries, a keen sense of observation, loving acceptance, and trust that the one who called us to ministry will continue to guide our paths in our first congregational call. If we train our senses to God's presence in our congregations, we will continually discover mysteries that surprise, confound, and inspire us as spiritual leaders.

The Wisdom of Opening the Door

I will conclude each chapter with words of wisdom and best practices gleaned from my work with new pastors and my more than thirty years of integrating academic and pastoral ministry. These words of wisdom are intended to provide best practices that a pastor can creatively adjust to her or his ministerial and personal setting.

CONNECT WITH COLLEAGUES

Virtually every new pastor notes the importance of healthy collegial relationships. Joanne describes her participation in a lectionary study group as invaluable in her first few years of

ministry: "What began as sharing our insights about the lectionary has become an opportunity for friendship and professional advice." A new pastor in Eastern Ohio, Steve appreciates
the monthly ecumenical gatherings of pastors in his area: "We
plan programs, but we also share our joys and challenges. It is
good to hear the wisdom of more experienced colleagues who
have survived what seems at the moment to be catastrophic to
me. It helps me keep things in perspective."

Lancaster Theological Seminary provides programs for
pastors in every season of ministry, especially during the first
few years of ministry. Pastors meet quarterly for daylong retreats that join prayer, checking in, theological education, and
Holy Communion.[7] Over the years, supportive friendships are
forged and ministerial wisdom is shared.

Some denominations assign mentors to newly ordained
ministers. Other new pastors seek out more experienced pastors for counsel as they take the first steps in their ministries.
The creative, confidential, and supportive relationship that is at
the heart of mentoring requires time and commitment on both
sides. A mentor's primary intention is to promote another's
well-being and spiritual growth, rather than a particular theological position, spiritual practice, or professional pathway.

Take Your Time

As a child, I learned the motto, "Stop, look, and listen." This
adage remains sage advice for new pastors. Trusting God's
guidance and movements in the world, we don't need to hurry
or immediately transform our congregations. In fact, tending
a congregation is like tending a garden: we need to take time
for the congregation to grow its gifts, providing just enough
guidance, challenge, and nurture for the congregation to flourish in partnership with its new pastor. To be effective spiritual
detectives and leaders, we need to let some things gently unfold
while actively promoting others. But as one pastor recalls, "I

avoided a lot of pitfalls simply by being still and not pushing things. Once I got to know the people and they got to know me, things really happened and we grew together."

Practice Self-Awareness

A key theme of my work in pastoral spirituality and excellence is inspired by Gerald May's spiritual counsel: *pause, notice, open, yield and stretch,* and *respond.* This wisdom applies to us as people and as congregational leaders. New pastors can cultivate self-awareness, knowing that while they cannot manage time or others' expectations, they can be intentional about their own lives and leadership. This self-awareness and self-monitoring involves holistic attention to body, mind, spirit, and relationships. In the spirit of the traditional examination of conscience, you might regularly ask yourself the following questions:

1. How is my overall well-being (body, mind, and spirit)?
2. Am I rested or stressed out?
3. Have I gained or lost weight in the last six months? If so, what was the reason for the changes?
4. Am I taking time for exercise, friendships, and self-care?
5. What is my attitude toward my congregants?
6. How do I feel about my sermon preparation?
7. How would I describe my prayer life and relationship with God?

Remember Your Family and Intimate Relationships

As I will discuss later, pastoral schedules are often difficult for spouses, partners, and children. While our families often look forward to weekends for relaxation, chores, and time together, these are often a pastor's busiest times. Conversely, pastors often take off weekdays, when their spouse or partner is working and the children are at school. Pastors need to be intentional about time with family, friends, and partners. Effective and healthy pastors are hard workers who also recognize that the flexibility of the pastoral schedule may give them unique opportunities to spend time with loved ones. This involves attentiveness to when and how we work, and the ability to say no to extraneous activities. Jonathan, a suburban Philadelphia pastor, notes the joy of "coming home in the afternoons to be with my young children." Steve has coached his son's Little League team, because he is one of few parents in his suburban D.C. neighborhood who can get off work most weekdays at 4:00 p.m. "Sure, I often have night meetings, but if I need to coach or go on a school field trip, I can take time to be with my children." This is especially important because Steve's spouse, an attorney, has less flexibility during the day than Steve's ministerial schedule affords.

Choosing when to spend time with family, friends, and other intimates involves awareness of the hours you work best and adjusting your professional schedule as much as possible to take advantage of the hours that are most productive for certain activities. For example, the majority of this text, and my nearly twenty books, was written before 9:00 a.m. As an early bird, I rise before 5:00 a.m. and after about ninety minutes of prayer, meditation, and walking, I write and study for two to three hours before heading to the seminary for administrative work, appointments, and teaching.

Recently, I discovered on a Facebook status update that one of my former Wesley Theological Seminary colleagues has a similar lifestyle. The mother of two young children pastoring a Presbyterian church in Georgia, Maggie posted that she was working on her sermon at 5:00 a.m.! This gives her time to be an emotionally present mother when her children wake up.

Pray without Ceasing

Starting with spirit is a dynamic process of call and response in which we train our senses to God's movements in our lives.

I believe that God is constantly calling us through inspiration, synchronicity, moments of clarity, helpful insights, and times of comfort and challenge. As Scripture tells us, Christ constantly stands at the door and knocks. We open the door to God's abundant life and professional guidance by taking time for stillness, prayers of petition and intercession, and moments of gratitude. While prayer can take many forms, the key is for new pastors to intentionally devote regular times each day to a prayerful relationship with the one who has begun and continues to do a good work in our lives.

CHAPTER 2

WHAT I DIDN'T LEARN IN SEMINARY, AND WHAT SEMINARIES CAN LEARN FROM NEW PASTORS

After three days [Mary and Joseph] found him in the temple, sitting among the teachers, listening to them and asking them questions. . . . And Jesus increased in wisdom and in years, and in divine and human favor.

—LUKE 2:46, 52

THE TRANSITION FROM SEMINARY TO YOUR FIRST CONGREgational call is similar to becoming a driver. If you want to drive a car, you must pass the written test, take driver training courses with an instructor, drive with a competent adult, and then head out on the open road on your own. You can't drive safely or skillfully without the preliminaries of instruction, classroom time, and mentoring behind the wheel, but—as every new driver knows, and best not forget—there is a quantum leap between driving with an instructor or your parents and taking your first solo drive. You can't wait to get your license, but that is only the beginning of the journey. A new driver still needs to become comfortable driving in traffic, navigating curves in the road, dealing with unanticipated hazards, discovering the right balance between caution and risk taking, and discerning the proper distance between moving vehicles. The new driver also needs to respond to other drivers in mature and respectful ways. Becoming a good driver takes time and is a matter of character and imagination as well as technical skill. Virtually every new driver is filled with fear and trembling when she first hits the road on her own.

Every new pastor goes through a similar process from the initial experience of being called to ministry, meeting with ministerial authorization bodies, taking courses in seminary, and then being called as a congregation's pastor. In the final year of seminary, most seminarians are eager to graduate. Like novice drivers, they yearn for the day when they can become congregational leaders. For many, the final seminary semester is almost intolerable. Like kids on the way to the beach, they keep asking, "Are we there yet? Can't we just speed up this process? I'm ready!"

Yet, like teenagers going out for their first solo drive, new pastors discover, as they open the doors to a new congregation and face the many firsts of ministry, that they still have a lot to learn. In reality, pastors are never "there yet." But over time and with a commitment to ongoing theological education and spiritual practices, novice pastors can embody the skills that lead to faithful excellence in ministry over a lifetime.

Over the past seven years, I have led spiritual formation and ministerial excellence groups involving nearly one hundred recent graduates of seminaries across the United States. All of them believe they received high quality seminary educations. Yet, all of them recognize that even the most comprehensive seminary education can't fully prepare them for the concrete realities of their first pastoral call. In this chapter, I will reflect on what these new pastors wish they had learned in seminary and ways seminaries might more creatively prepare new pastors for navigating the transition from seminary to their first congregational call.

What New Pastors Wish They Had Learned in Seminary

At a recent lunch gathering with six pastors serving in their first few years of ministry, I asked the question, "Now that you've been in the parish for a while, what do you wish you'd learned in seminary?" The first response of these graduates from Lancaster Theological Seminary and Moravian Theological Seminary, most of whom are now studying in Lancaster's Doctor of Ministry program, was to give their seminaries high marks for their courses in theology, pastoral care, church history, and Scripture. Then, they got down to the business of reflecting on how seminary might have been more helpful in preparing them for their first congregational position.

Each one of these high functioning pastors as well as dozens of others with whom I have met over the past several years responded, "Seminary prepared me well to understand the big picture issues of theology and pastoral care, but not the everyday nuts and bolts of ministry." Now "nuts and bolts" may mean different things to different pastors, but most new pastors lift up issues such as: how to do a wedding rehearsal, keep ministerial records (wedding and funeral), understand income tax regulations for clergy, run a stewardship campaign, or even discuss the practice of stewardship effectively in their congregations.

Nuts-and-bolts issues can make or break a congregation and a minister's professional life. They involve the *how* of ministry, the daily tasks of ministry that enable us to embody the pastoral imagination. Although most pastors do not initially see administration at the heart of their pastoral call, they soon come to realize that without effective administration, the foundations of church life eventually collapse, regardless of the quality of their sermons or pastoral care.[1] Joe, the pastor of a United Church

of Christ congregation near Reading, Pennsylvania, wishes he
had learned more about the business of the church in seminary.
When Joe first arrived at his congregation, he found that the financial records were in shambles. "I spent much of my first year
at the church reading books on standard financial procedures
for congregations. Only then did I feel comfortable addressing the financial problems I observed." Another pastor with an
accounting background prior to attending seminary was both
amazed and depressed when she proofread the congregation's
stewardship letter and proposed budget. She comments, "The
financial report, which accompanied the letter, included pen-
ciled in annotations, misspelled words, and financial inaccura-
cies. I had to go over the document line by line with the chair
of the board and treasurer before I allowed the letter to be sent
out." In reflecting on the apparent dissonance between her call
to ministry and the details of everyday life, this pastor notes:

> When I experienced God calling me to ordained ministry,
> I thought it primarily involved preaching, pastoral care, and
> prayer. I never thought that my accounting and administra-
> tive skills would be central to my pastoral leadership. At first,
> I was angry at how much time I spent on the business details
> of the church, but now I'm grateful for my first career and feel
> sorry for pastors who have no business training prior to com-
> ing to seminary.

Virtually every pastor begins her first congregational call unaware of the administrative complexities of congregational personnel issues. Nearly half of the new pastors in the Wholeness
in Ministry program, who serve in congregations with fewer
than two hundred members, report arriving in a congregation
in which the church secretary is a long-time member and often
the spouse of a major leader in the church. Many of these sec-
retaries have little or no knowledge of current office technolo-
gies, believe they run the congregation, and often are guilty of

serious boundary violations related to confidentiality. Virtually none of them have written job descriptions or procedures for performance reviews. In such circumstances, personnel issues are truly personal for both the pastor and the congregation. Poorly handled personnel issues can end a pastor's honeymoon before it begins. As one pastor notes, "I had no idea what to do when I realized how dysfunctional the office situation was. I needed some first steps to resolve the situation, and the required courses in seminary never told me how to run an effective church office." Others arrive in congregations with no secretary at all and have to cobble together a volunteer staff or become their own secretary—printing bulletins, handling the mail, and answering the phone.

In our book, *From a Mustard Seed: Enlivening Worship and Music in the Small Church*, Lancaster Theological Seminary's Dean of the Chapel Daryl Hollinger and I reflect on the question, "Pastor and Church Musician—Friend, Foe, or Fiasco?" From our experiences as church musician and pastor respectively, we know how important a healthy partnership can be in creating meaningful worship services.[2] One of the most important congregational personnel issues involves the questions, Who plans worship? and How are the hymns and liturgies chosen? When Ruthann, a graduate of Moravian Seminary, asserted, "Seminary never told me how to get along with musicians," every pastor in our session nodded his or her head. I suspect a group of church musicians might make a similar comment about working with pastors. In describing his worship class, a United Methodist pastor recalled:

> We learned a great deal about the liturgies and hymnody of the church, but we learned nothing about how to lead a worship planning team. Group worship planning—and really I want group input—has been my greatest headache in ministry. I want to know how I can guide congregational worship and yet be sensitive to the feelings of the choir director.

Good pastors join the quest for excellence in congregational life and worship with attention to healthy personnel relationships. Personnel issues always involve relationships with people! They also involve bringing together in a creative way diverse visions of worship and administration. Most pastors struggle to hold fast to their vision of faithful excellence in ministry and yet respond lovingly to imperfections and conflicts involving church staff and laypeople. Balancing faithful excellence with pastoral sensitivity becomes especially challenging when a beloved organist of more than fifty years can no longer do her job. A Congregationalist minister in New Hampshire, Carol recalls several painful meetings with board members regarding one such organist:

> We were poised to grow in our changing [town-and-country] neighborhood. Young families were coming to church, but after enduring our congregation's depressing music, few ever returned. I wished someone had given me guidance in seminary about how to lovingly tell someone who is no longer competent that he or she needs to resign.

A United Church of Christ pastor in Eastern Pennsylvania, Bud echoes these comments in his counsel that seminaries spend more time exploring practical issues new pastors will face in their first congregational call. Although he is grateful for his seminary training at Lutheran Theological Seminary at Philadelphia, he believes

> seminary education needs to give more time to practical issues and less to the theoretical and theological aspects of ministry. Courses—and not just one theoretical course but hands-on practice—in conflict management and mediation are crucial, both for work within the church [and] in the community. I've taken one retreat on conflict management, but that just isn't enough. I find it interesting . . . that I am getting a good

education in conflict management through secular avenues, such as serving on the social inclusion committee at my daughter's school.

While I personally believe that more, rather than less, theology needs to be taught in seminaries given the rapidly changing pluralistic, postmodern, and post-Christian world in which we live, I also affirm the importance of helping students apply theological concepts to the everyday situations in the community and in congregational life. As one new pastor confesses, "I keep most of my theological insights to myself. I still read books in theology and biblical studies but struggle to share their insights with my parishioners. I need to find a way to share good scholarship in ways that edify, and not initially offend, my fairly traditional congregation." Another newly ordained pastor asked with more than a little frustration, "When I use words like *eschatology* or *synoptic*, I can see their eyes glazing over. How do I talk about theology and the Bible the way I learned it in seminary in ways my congregation can understand?" Translating the faith we affirm as pastors into the everyday language of congregants applies to every aspect of ministry. We may begin with the sermon, but we also share why theology makes a difference in shaping the church's budget, outreach to the community, or response to a conflict within the congregation. All theology is intended to be *practical theology* insofar as it influences the values and practices of personal and congregational life.

Practical theological reflection is crucial for effective preaching over the long haul. Most recent seminary graduates find the task of weekly preaching challenging, to say the least. This is a matter of not only translating theological concepts into everyday language but also learning to preach an innovative and inspiring word forty-five to fifty weeks each year. Even the most effective preaching courses require only a handful of sermons in the course of a semester. As Sarah, an ELCA pastor, admits: "In seminary, I spent twenty hours preparing for each of the two sermons I preached in my homiletics class. Now that I'm preaching every week—and sometimes twice a week in Advent, Lent, Holy Week, and Easter—I barely get five hours to prepare for each week's sermon, and that's on a good week. I haven't found a way to pace myself so that I can preach effectively and do all the other tasks of ministry."[3] Tom, a United Methodist pastor, mirrors Sarah's concern: "As a solo pastor, I sometimes preach twenty weeks in a row without a break. I enjoy preaching and like to study for sermons. But sometimes I wish that I'd been assigned to an associate position, where I could really prepare for my monthly sermon. Sometimes the best I can do in a busy week is to look at online commentaries like textweek.com and the *Christian Century* for inspiration and examples." Regular preaching involves the creative use of time, maximizing quiet weeks to get ahead in preparation, and learning helpful shortcuts for those weeks when unexpected deaths and crises undermine the best laid plans for sermon preparation.

Translating theology in worship and preaching involves the creative use of media and the spoken and written word. Over the past several years, dozens of pastors have lamented, in more or less the same words: "My congregation wants to do more contemporary worship and use the Internet for outreach, and so do I, but the seminary's only communication classes focused on writing and preaching. Most of my professors acted as if using the Internet and data projectors in worship and preaching somehow compromised our theological integrity as pastors and scholars."

Another common concern that I have heard from new pastors is that although seminary prepares them for leading relatively healthy and financially stable congregations, they receive little training for guiding the struggling and often dysfunctional congregations that they may be called to serve. Often new pastors are called to the most financially and organizationally troubled congregations and have few resources for leading congregations through budget shortfalls, diminishing membership, political controversies, and much-needed change. In addition, new pastors from cities and suburban areas are shocked when they discover the intricate familial relationships in many rural and small town congregations. Carol recalls her shock one Sunday morning when she looked out at her congregation and realized that nearly "everyone belonged to one of three extended families. At that moment, I recognized that when I ministered to one person, I indirectly ministered to fifty, and that family feuds found their way into the dynamics of church board meetings and Sunday school classes." I suspect that this neglect in the seminary curriculum is more a matter of omission rather than intention on the part of seminary professors, most of whom attend more intellectually sophisticated and relationally diverse city or suburban congregations. Still, the concern is valid, especially given the radical difference in the dynamics and expectations articulated by rural and city congregations. Nowhere is this difference more obvious than in pastoral care. As one small town Disciples of Christ pastor notes:

> I was raised in a midsized city where people didn't expect the pastor to visit their homes. The pastor often met people for lunch or at the Starbucks. Here in Western Pennsylvania, they expect their pastor to come by their homes for a piece of pie or supper. If I'd been taught in seminary about different church cultures and how they shape congregants' expectations, I would have avoided a lot of problems in the first few months of ministry.

Many new pastors wish they had learned how to balance the many and varied tasks of ministry during their seminary studies. Ministerial stress and the use of time are closely connected. The habits we learn or perpetuate in seminary regarding personal well-being, relationships, and self-care will follow us into our first congregational call. Susan asserts, "Seminary gives mixed messages about self-care. On the one hand, everyone says, 'Take care of yourself and your family first,' but sometimes I think each professor acts as if her or his class is the only one we're taking. How can I read four hundred pages, go to my field education assignment, work part time to help pay the bills, and be a good mother and wife? Life only gets more complicated in the parish!" Another high-functioning pastor recalls, "I got on the 24/7 treadmill in seminary, and I haven't been able to get off. I wish someone had told me how to decide what's really important and what I can let go of for a while. Right now, everything seems important, and I don't have any criteria for decision-making."

In that same spirit, most new pastors complain about not having enough time to pursue excellence in ministry, self-care, and family life. As one of the few remaining professional generalists, pastors use a variety of often contrasting skill sets in the course of the day. They may go from a property maintenance issue to pastoral calls, work on the newsletter, look for medical resources for the Bhutanese family the church is sponsoring through Church World Service, take a look at next Sunday's scriptures, counsel the children of a senior adult with Alzheimer's disease, and plan a youth retreat—all in the course of one day. Therefore, *how* we work is often as important for overall ministerial well-being as what we do. Rather than practicing the generalist approach necessary for effective ministry, most seminary professors are specialists who don't always present a clear connection between their discipline and the everyday realities of ministry. As one seminarian laments, "On only a few occasions did a faculty member show us how to juggle the many tasks of ministry without dropping everything. I wished I'd learned more about how Calvin, Luther, and Wesley managed to put it all together in their professional lives and how their professional commitments shaped their lifestyle and family life. I would have liked to hear how their wives felt about their ministries!"

While most new pastors are grateful for the solid foundation that a good seminary education provides, they also recognize the limitations of an education that often fails to connect coursework with issues of ministerial practice, pastoral decision-making, self-care, and the nuts and bolts necessary for effective ministry. Today's seminaries need to listen to the voices of their graduates and their congregations and then creatively respond with courses that explicitly join theological reflection and practical application in ministry.

The Seminary as a Seedbed of Possibilities

Philosopher Alfred North Whitehead believed that the capacity to respond imaginatively to environmental change is a unique characteristic of human beings. The philosopher's call to creative transformation challenges seminaries and pastors to innovatively integrate theory and practice in theological education. I am fond of quoting the line, "The railroads went out of business because they thought that their business was railroads and not transportation." Then I add that for seminaries to embody their vocation today, they must see their business as providing theological resources and education for congregations and laypeople in addition to seminary students. Seminaries have often forgotten that their vocation as well as their institutional well-being is intimately connected to the well-being of congregations. I believe that seminaries best fulfill their vocation of training congregational leaders when they also attend to the needs of the congregations that these future leaders will serve. Grounded in my conversations with dozens of pastors, my suggestions for transforming seminary education advocate a return to holistic approaches characteristic of earlier centuries but adapted to address particular twenty-first century challenges.

In their quest to provide holistic and effective theological education for the twenty-first century, in every class and in the curriculum as a whole, the seminary community needs to ask continually, So what? How does this course promote faithful excellence in ministry and professional life? How does the subject matter and teaching technique contribute to revitalizing the church and to transformational leadership? While theology as a discipline of the church's life is at the heart of seminary education, theological education, including church history and biblical studies, must be understood as practical as well as theoretical in nature. Only in the past few centuries have seminaries separated theory and practice. Major theologians in the past and many present theologians forged their theology in daily dialogue with congregational life. Martin Luther, Ulrich Zwingli, John Calvin, John Wesley, Friedrich Schleiermacher, Reinhold Niebuhr, and Howard Thurman filled pulpits as well as classrooms. Their integration of theology and practical ministry inspired them to explore new possibilities for theological reflection and congregational leadership appropriate to their times and places.

The word *seminary* is rooted in the concept of a seedbed. Seminaries, at their best, are seedbeds of possibility from which faithful, effective, and transformational leadership emerges. For the past several years, I have contended that vital theological education involves the interplay of vision, promise, and practice. Seminaries help students and congregations formulate their theological visions, affirm that these theological visions can be experienced in life-transforming ways, and teach practices to nurture the experience of God's movement in our world. From this perspective, even the most erudite theological theory or ancient text invites future pastors to make connections with congregational life as it is and as it could be. For example, in my course on process theology, an otherwise esoteric subject, I explore the importance of our vision of God for the practices of preaching, congregational leadership, spiritual formation, church administration, and pastoral care, often all in the same class session. If tradition involves embracing the most lively insights and practices of prior generations, then every century of Christian history should be applied to current issues of congregational vitality and pastoral leadership. The context and methodology change, as do the realities of congregational life, but the vision that people and communities will be transformed and made whole still serves as the polestar for congregational life.

Every seminary course has pastoral implications. Brick-and-mortar issues of administration reflect our attitudes toward stewardship and the presence of God in the material world. Systematic theology shapes preaching, administration, worship, and pastoral care, and the connections need to be clearly made. Church history courses can highlight how theological challenges of the past are still alive in our congregations and can consider how the responses of major Christian figures are still valuable in shaping our own ministerial responses.

The process of translation needs to be modeled in the classroom first, with questions such as: Does it preach? If not, what is the impediment? If so, how do I preach it from the pulpit or teach it in a church school class? Or: How will this help me more creatively respond to the culture of my congregation or respond to the challenges of congregational leadership? It is not that these questions are absent from seminaries. They simply need to be made explicit and essential to every class session. Academic scholarship is essential to the life of the seminary, but pastors need to bring together the pulpit, classroom, and hospital room in their professional lives.

The holistic nature of theological education is evident in the pastor's role as congregational theologian. The rabbinical or teaching role of the pastor is grounded in the pastoral imagination, which sees all things in light of God's presence and then seeks to respond to God's movement in every pastoral encounter. Therefore, making connections between theory and practice must be at the heart of theological education. Along with mastering the theological and scriptural vocabulary, seminarians need to learn ways to explain complex terms in the everyday language of the people they serve.

Practical issues, such as those to which Bud alluded earlier in this chapter, can be addressed effectively in theology, ethics, Scripture, and pastoral care classes and in courses focusing specifically on congregational systems, conflict management, and administration. Concern for congregational vitality, outreach, and transformation should be implicit, and often explicit, in seminary courses. Becky, a high functioning associate minister in Hagerstown, Maryland, affirms:

> I wished I had learned more about revitalizing churches. The congregation I serve is an older church with 150-plus years of history to navigate. We aren't dead yet, but we are seriously in need of some vitality. To compensate for what I didn't learn in seminary, I've been reading about church vitality, attending continuing education events related to this topic, and trying to learn from congregations and pastors who are experiencing new growth and life.

Becky's comments challenge seminaries to provide resources for congregations and pastors who are called to transformational ministries. Innovative and effective pastors can partner with seminary faculty in seamlessly integrating theory and practice for congregational growth and transformation. The presence of ministerial practitioners in the seminary faculty will add concrete experience to seminary courses in preaching, congregational life, and administration and to traditional courses in theology and church history. Skilled practitioners may regularly be invited as guest lecturers in required theology, ethics, preaching, pastoral care, worship, and administration courses for the sole purpose of making connections between theory and practice and to show how pastors can use what they learn in seminary in daily tasks of ministry and congregational life.

While most seminaries are currently revamping their field education, or internship, programs, a simple but effective approach to field education for seminarians would involve creating a checklist of ministerial tasks that ideally need to be accomplished in the course of the year. Learning these ministerial tasks would begin with observation, followed by supervised practice, and then (when possible) opportunities for the seminarian to take the lead. While some of these tasks may involve observation rather than hands-on involvement, a congregational field education checklist might include the following:

Conducting weddings and wedding rehearsals
Preparing for funerals
Reading financial records
Prioritizing ministerial tasks
Dealing with conflict situations
Learning insights helpful for preaching every week, including weekly lectionary reading
Dealing with a building maintenance issues
Managing office procedures
Planning worship
Managing time
Understanding clergy taxes

The goal in seminary courses is to promote healthy and effective ministry. Ministry is a whole-person enterprise, and faithful excellence in ministry involves connecting heart, mind, and hands. In the spirit of the Benedictine Order, today's seminaries need to provide theological and spiritual undergirding for everything a pastor does as well as the training to embody these theological principles in the quotidian tasks of ministry.

Creative Wisdom for Theological Education

From my numerous conversations with both seminarians and new pastors, the primary wisdom I have to offer seminary students is to begin to claim your leader's voice. Seminary education is a progression in which students learn the basics of their craft—intellectually and, we hope, experientially. While we are always learners, most educational pedagogies implicitly encourage passivity rather than the activity necessary for effective ministerial leadership. For this reason, I encourage my students, as a best practice in theological education, to make a sharp turn from passive to active voice during their second year in seminary. Such a turn can be as subtle as constantly asking, "What do I think of this?" or "How will I translate this to a congregation?" after adequately digesting a reading assignment.

Another best practice in claiming your pastoral voice is to constantly ask the question, "So what?" not as a challenge to your professors but as a way of making the connection between theory and practice, even if your professor fails to do so. My primary rationale for counseling students to make the turn from passive to active during seminary is that claiming your own voice, albeit in the humble spirit of Jeremiah, prepares you for the first time a congregant asks, "What do you think, pastor?" In such moments, they aren't interested in what John Cobb, Mary Daly, Jurgen Moltmann, or Paul Tillich thinks, although their insights are invaluable to pastoral ministry. They want to know where you stand as their spiritual leader, whether on a Sunday school curriculum or the ethics of marriage equality.

Practicing your active voice is part of the critical discernment and pastoral imagination necessary for creative and faithful ministry. Other pathways to the active voice include reflecting on your personal credo yearly during seminary and updating your credo in your first years in ministry following seminary. Ask yourself on a yearly basis questions such as, How do I understand God's presence in the world? The Holy Spirit? The power of prayer? The goal is not to construct a rigid theology but to affirm your deepest beliefs. Then, ask yourself, What difference do these beliefs make in my life? How do I live them out in daily life and decision making?

In seminary, it is important that students learn the rhythm of pastoral leadership along with the rhythm of academic life.

For example, in preparation for preaching as many as fifty sermons a year, I suggest that during their seminary years future pastors spend an hour, in two sittings, reflecting on the weekly lectionary, again with a set of questions such as, What is the scripture saying to me? How might I share this insight with a congregation? What difference would taking these seriously make in the lives of my future congregants? Here, the goal is not to write a sermon but to begin to think homiletically in a holistic fashion by joining theory and practice, and overcoming the divide between spirituality and religion experienced by many seekers. In *Tending to the Holy*, Kate Epperly and I describe a number of practices that join spirituality and sermon preparation. We have found certain practices such as *lectio divina*, or holy reading; imaginative prayers; and walking prayer helpful in inspiring homiletic creativity and inspiration.

Wise seminarians eventually realize that they must take responsibility for their spiritual lives, physical well-being, and attitudes toward time, the issues addressed in chapter 1.[4] A number of seminaries, such as Lancaster Theological Seminary, teach the practices of praying the hours, centering prayer, and the examen of conscience as part of group spiritual formation classes. Perhaps a good place to start is simply with a breath prayer that can be practiced in sitting meditation or in the course of daily activities. As you breathe, open yourself to God's Spirit moving through your life, and experience God's Spirit centering, calming, and revitalizing your whole being. Imagine that Jesus is breathing in and through you as he did with the disciples that first Easter (John 20:22).

Effective and excellent ministry involves being intentional about your schedule and priorities. Time and stress are closely connected in ministry, and I will address these issues more fully in a later chapter. Many pastors rush from one task to the other without considering their well-being or their goals in the various tasks of ministry. They may eventually come to suffer from what physician Larry Dossey describes as time sickness or hurry sickness. While pastors can never fully manage time, they can creatively shape their experience of time—even with the reality of unexpected events—through meditation and intentional rhythms of rest and activity, by pursuing hobbies and time with family, and by working on sermons in advance during slow ministerial weeks. Advent, Lent, and Easter don't have to catch pastors by surprise. We can prepare for the seasons of the church so that the extra services and sermons don't overwhelm us or diminish the quality of our ministries or family lives.

CHAPTER 3

AUTHORITY AND RELATIONSHIP IN THE CHURCH

Then Jesus said to Simon, "Do not be afraid; from now on you will be catching people." When they had brought their boats to shore, they left everything and followed him.

—LUKE 5:10–11

WHEN I ASKED SUSAN, THE SOLO PASTOR OF A UNITED Church of Christ congregation in Central Pennsylvania, to describe what gives her authority in ministry, her response was thoughtful but bold: "My training and my call to ministry." She elaborated, "My training and ongoing study give me the authority to apply the Scriptures to daily life in the pulpit or the classroom." But Susan's ongoing sense of call also arises from her experience of being touched by God. As she asserts, "I can't *not* be a pastor."

Susan's sense of call, like that of the prophets Jeremiah and Isaiah, joins mysticism and ministry. Late one night, while working as a fund-raiser for a public broadcasting station,

Susan heard a voice from a place deeper than consciousness say to her, "There's a bigger meaning in life than fund-raising." Although she was an agnostic at the time, Susan decided to attend church that next week. On her first Sunday back in church, she heard another voice calling from within her: "I want you to come home. I want you to heal the church." Susan became involved in the congregation, growing in faith and confidence, gradually claiming her gifts for ministry by studying at a local lay ministry school. Over several months, her inner sense of call was complemented by a chorus of personal affirmations calling her to go to seminary.

In her journey toward claiming God's call to spiritual leadership, she shared her growing call with the senior pastor of her church, who discouraged her, telling her she didn't have what it takes to make it in seminary and lacked the gifts of ministry. Initially devastated, Susan considered abandoning her plan until another voice from deep within interceded, reminding her, "You're a child of God. Trust God. Period!" That inner certainty, plus the ongoing affirmation from laypeople and other clergy, helped Susan claim her call to heal the church as an ordained minister. Susan recalls that she excelled in seminary through a lot of prayer and hard work.

Today, as she leads her small town congregation through a time of revitalization, Susan affirms, "God was at work, guiding me through gentle nudges, even when I was an agnostic. The call to ministry doesn't come from us alone: it's from God and the voices of others who see God's work in our lives." Today, Susan still trusts God to guide her ministry. Theologically grounded in process theology and its open-ended, possibility-oriented, and noncoercive vision of God, church, and ministry, Susan still listens for God's gentle movements in her life. She believes that the Spirit is present in her sermon preparation as well as her preaching. "God's inspiration is everywhere, even when I don't feel particularly inspired as I study the lectionary texts." Susan admits that she often has "no clear idea what this sermon's going to be about, even after I've spent the week studying. I've done my preparation, but I know that I need God's guidance to bring it to the pulpit." Susan's authority comes from her sense of the Spirit as well as her preparation, that is, by inspiration as well as perspiration!

As I pondered Susan's sense of call and authority, I was reminded that although God calls everyone to service, God invites certain people to take pastoral leadership within congregations. The apostle Paul recognizes that all Christians are gifted for ministry, but that some Christians are uniquely called to equip the saints, that is, to inspire and challenge others to embody God's vocation for them in the community and the world (Eph. 4:12). Many experience a gentle and gradual inclination over time that leads them to enroll in seminary. Others, like St. Augustine—and Susan—experience a dramatic call to ministry, hear a voice that says, "Take and read," and then open themselves to God's guidance in Scripture. Although God calls all creation toward wholeness, God calls each person to embody God's vision of shalom through her or his gifts, talents, and experiences. Although I do not believe that God plans the details of our lives or acts in our lives apart from our input, I affirm that God nevertheless guides many people toward following the call to spiritual leadership in the church.[1]

With the sense of call comes authority in ministry. In fact, call and authority are interdependent and constantly evolving in relation to God's universal call to all creation and humankind; God's personal and vocational callings moment by moment and over the course of our lives; God's call within a community that recognizes our unique gifts toward ministry and spiritual leadership; and the call of church bodies, denominations and congregations, that authorize a pastor's ministry in its particular context. As pastors and communities of faith ponder the nature of ministerial call and authority, it is important that they keep at least three things in mind: (1) God calls everyone in the congregation and not just the pastor to fulfill her or his call. (2) The pastor, like all of us, has more than one call in her or his life and is not called only to ordained ministry. (God calls through our families and relationships, overall health condition, and social context, not just through the church and its vocation.) And (3) the calls of pastors and congregations evolve over time. Still, from the very beginning of human history, certain people—medicine women and men, shamans, prophets, priests, magi—have been set apart by their encounter with the Holy, despite any impediments they have seen in fulfilling their vocations. For example, Moses, for all his physical, experiential, and emotional challenges, was called by God to bring hope and direction to an oppressed people. Peter was called at the workplace to go deeper in his vocation, to expand his vision of fishing to include transforming people's spiritual lives. Mary of Magdala was called in her grief to share the good news of resurrection to Jesus's distraught followers. Today's new pastors are the spiritual children of those whom Jesus called by the lakeside, embodying that call and discovering their authority as leaders for their time and place. They can claim their call and understand and use that authority as congregational leaders in a variety of ways.

Authority for Transformation

Darryl is the pastor of an inner city Reading, Pennsylvania, United Church of Christ congregation rooted in the liturgical tradition of the German Reformed Church. As he reflected with me on the nature of authority, Darryl recalled a saying that characterized his relational approach to leadership: "They don't care what you know until they know that you care." Darryl, who is Hispanic, is still amazed that a very traditional, all-white congregation called him as its pastor when he was just twenty-six. More surprising was the fact that before coming to the United Church of Christ, Darryl's religious journey involved integrating Roman Catholic and Pentecostal faith traditions. Both traditions give their pastors tremendous authority and assume that they are set apart from the rest of the congregation in spiritually unique ways. Darryl noted that in his Pentecostal congregation, "The pastor had sole authority and made every important decision." He soon, and happily, discovered that authority is understood quite differently in the United Church of Christ: "I don't have to make every decision; responsibility is shared." The church, which had been placed on "hospice care" by some observers, reached out to this young pastor, as Darryl said, "taking me under its wings and showing me the ropes. This allowed me to move from being a learner to becoming their pastor." Darryl has been a change agent, bringing new life to this struggling congregation by beginning a congregation-based afterschool program, reaching out to the growing international community in the neighborhood, and becoming a chaplain on the police force. Darryl recalled that initially "I didn't think it would last too long, but now I've been there six years, and we love each other."

Darryl's sense of call and the authority that goes with it is biblical and relational. Darryl affirmed, "A called man or woman of God needs to take ownership of the call. As called ministers, we have to speak the truth of the gospel even if this means taking a stand that differs from our people." Darryl continued, "If it's my responsibility to lead, I use the power vested in me by the congregation and the larger church."

For Darryl, given his strong Pentecostal roots, the pastor is called to be differentiated and, at times, prophetic, in his or her approach to leadership. According to Darryl, "You can't just reflect the beliefs and practices of your congregation. How I respond to certain issues and how I claim authority involves an ongoing process of prayerful discernment, making sure it's the higher voice, God's voice, which is always bigger than our plans or my ego." Darryl recognizes that God calls individuals, but God's call is always, as Darryl noted, "larger than us, and challenging us to see a bigger picture than our understanding of what the congregation can be." Although Darryl sees his call as coming from God's presence in his life, he also tries to encourage the congregation to claim its own experiences of God's guidance. "It's not my church and not just my vision. I would like the congregation to have more young people and be more liberal politically, but the call is bigger than my vision, and that keeps me humble."

Joyce, an African American woman who pastors a primarily European American United Methodist congregation in the Philadelphia suburbs, concurs with Darryl's recognition that pastoral authority, while personal in nature, must ultimately lie with God. "For me the Bible, the First and Second Testament, are authorities for my leadership. My congregation knows that my position and role is based on Scripture."

Like Darryl and Joyce, Bonnie, the pastor of a United Church of Christ congregation in Lancaster, believes call, authority, relationship, and theology go hand in hand. When she was called to be pastor of this church just a block from Lancaster Theological Seminary, she was told by the search committee that they needed "a tough administrator, strong preacher, and someone to grow the church." With many years of experience in program administration, development, and public relations prior to entering the ministry, Bonnie recognized that her gifts met their needs, and she took their mandate to heart. As she states, "I assume that this is what I am supposed to do, and I will go ahead and do it, to respond to the church's mission." Bonnie is not afraid to confront an issue from the pulpit or in a committee meeting. "I need to preach the gospel. The Bible's pretty clear about certain things, and often I come to the pulpit saying, 'This is tough, and I wish I could make it easy on you, but this will hurt some.'" But even on the most challenging passages, Bonnie always remembers to include a word of good news and affirmation.

Bonnie recalls a humorous opportunity for asserting her authority in the church. Under Bonnie's leadership, St. Peter's has initiated a number of programs oriented to the community—classes for refugees new to the Lancaster area and a 12-step group. At one property meeting, controversy arose when a number of members noted, "They're stealing our toilet paper." Bonnie asked the group to look beyond the issue of toilet paper and reflect on why rolls of toilet paper might be missing from the restrooms. The group's wisdom was that the people needed toilet paper and couldn't afford it. Bonnie asked them if they really wanted to lock up the toilet paper and suggested an alternative, leaving a few rolls out for the taking. As Bonnie jokes, "The one thing we have in this church is lots of toilet paper." Needless to say, the problem has disappeared.

Bonnie notes that the biblical tradition is clear about what behaviors are appropriate and inappropriate for Christians, and that she doesn't tolerate "muck and gossip in the church." Still, when she needs to confront an unhealthy behavior, she begins by reaching out to the identified offender. "Often people complain because they want to be heard, but people don't listen to them because they constantly complain. I need to stop this vicious cycle. I listen first and then challenge the behavior on biblical grounds."

Carolene, a United Methodist associate pastor serving in the Philadelphia suburbs, asserts that pastoral authority is multidimensional. "The position itself, the training, the commissioning, the ordination all contribute to my authority as a pastor." She recognizes that authority is more than functional. It is transformational, spiritual, and personal in ways that set pastors apart: "Something really happened when the bishop laid hands on me at my ordination. I felt a weight and a power." Carolene believes that authority also "comes from integrity and character, and how we go about being pastors. My passion is to empower the laity. This isn't about manipulation but tapping into their passion; feeding the fire of their passion. My sense of shared pastoral authority inspires me to provide what they need to live out their passion as Christians."

Carolene's approach to authority embodies the spirit of the body of Christ described in 1 Corinthians 12. Claiming a holistic and relational understanding of authority, she sees the pastor as a key figure in nurturing the church's well-being by nurturing the gifts of individuals and groups within the congregation. The task of equipping the saints involves sharing power rather than hoarding it. While some pastors have a zero-sum, win-lose approach to authority, viewing any gain in power by the laity as a loss for the pastor, Carolene understands authority as supportive and empowering: "My authority is relational, inspirational, and supportive. It's an authority of care in which I seek to provide what they need to act on their passions for ministry."

In a similar fashion, Chris, a Central Pennsylvania Presbyterian pastor, sees her authority as joining character and theological reflection. According to Chris, who is a student of congregational systems theory, "My authority comes from being a nonanxious presence. Systems theory gives me a larger perspective on what's going on at church. This enables me to have a sense of peace amid change and the anticipated resistance to change."[2] Claiming her vocation as the primary theologian of her congregation, Chris belives one of her responsibilities is to remind the congregation, when it gets caught up in the values and behaviors of the surrounding culture, what it means to be a Christian in today's world. Like the apostle Paul, Chris and other new pastors remind their congregations to be transformed by God, rather than conformed to the world's values (Rom. 12:2).

Karen, a Mennonite pastor, found Christian educator and congregational consultant Celia Hahn's text *Growing in Authority, Relinquishing Control* instrumental in finding her voice as the called spiritual leader in her congregation.[3] Although she follows the servant leader approach to ministry and emphasizes the importance of shared leadership, Karen recognizes that her authority as pastor involves protecting the congregation's well-being when inappropriate behaviors threaten its mission as the body of Christ. Her sense of call and commitment to congregational health requires her to stand alone from time to time as the one who shares God's vision for the church. Like Chris, Karen is aware of how congregants' behaviors, positive or negative, shape the overall health of the church. Karen and Chris exemplify Jackson Carroll's belief that "the primary task of leaders, ordained or lay, remains that of ensuring the congregation's identity as the body of Christ in ways that are appropriate to its particular culture and context."[4]

Faith, the pastor of a family-size United Methodist Church on the Chesapeake Bay, affirms that being set apart is essential to pastoral authority. Also a student of congregational systems theory, Faith notes that "80 percent of the people in my church are related to one another and have established roles, behaviors, and ways of relating to one another that they bring to church." Faith asserts that being an outsider gives the pastor the authority that comes from being relationally differentiated:

> The pastor may be expected to ignore bad behavior, because that's "just how Sally is," or to keep an incompetent leader on the board because "we don't want to hurt him. The church is all he has." As an outside person, the pastor can actually be more effective in addressing problems within the church because (1) she has outside authority, (2) she is not "one of us," and (3) she can serve as a scapegoat—she can have the hard conversation that everyone wants to have but cannot because of their role in the family system.

Faith recognizes the reality that in spite of their attempts to challenge a pastor's self-differentiation, congregations ultimately want their pastors to be set apart and to hold them to God's larger vision for the church. As Steve, another Maryland United Methodist pastor states, "They need me to mirror their concerns, but they also tell me that they want me to challenge their ways of doing things, even when they push back. I have learned that if I listen and honor their experience, they are willing to question their own images of the church and its mission."[5]

Still, Faith and other new pastors recognize that the pastor's outsider status can also be problematic. "I have authority as the pastor of a United Methodist church, but if everyone knows certain congregational secrets or information I'm not privy to, then my authority and ability to act appropriately is undercut." Faith recognizes that even the most insightful pastor may unknowingly put the well-being of the church at risk because she is "not given essential information by either congregational leaders or denominational officials." More than a few pastors admitted that their churches hid issues of substance abuse, mental health, and sexual impropriety that undercut their ability to exercise effective pastoral leadership within the congregation.

Ray, a United Church of Christ pastor of two village congregations in Central Pennsylvania, works hard to ensure his authority is relational and team oriented. This, however, is not easy, since in many congregations in the German Reformed branch of the United Church of Christ, the primary model of ministry is that of "Herr Pastor," which, as Ray says, maintains that "the pastor is the primary authority on everything from interpreting the Word of God to the sound system." His predecessor and many other previous pastors made "all the important decisions and did everything," according to Ray. Although the pastor had great authority in the Herr Pastor model, this model, Ray believes, "severely disempowers the laity, such that anything beyond maintenance issues in the church becomes the pastor's work." Ray has tried to remedy this, with some success, by creating a "team situation in which the pastor is just one of the team players, whose vocation is to help them discover their own wisdom and expertise."

As he considers the nature of God's call to everyone within the church, Ray affirms, "God's voice doesn't speak just to me but also to my congregants." He hopes that his two congregations will recognize God's call to them, which will result in a full partnership that will enable him to live out his vocation as spiritual leader who seeks to equip his flocks to embrace their own roles as ministers within the body of Christ.

A Theology of Call and Authority

Most pastors recognize the need for a theology of call and authority for the practice of ministry, be it lay or ordained. They recognize that they are set apart as pastors and teachers within the church to "equip the saints for the work of ministry, for the building up of the body of Christ . . . to maturity, to the measure of the full stature of Christ" (Eph. 4:12–13). As *The Book of Common Prayer* of the Episcopal Church asserts, people seeking ordination are "called to work as a pastor, priest, and teacher . . . to proclaim by word and deed the Gospel of Jesus Christ, . . . to preach, to declare God's forgiveness to penitent sinners, to pronounce God's blessing, to share in the administration of Holy Baptism and in the celebration of the mysteries of Christ's Body and Blood."[6] In the United Church of Christ, the "Service of Ordination to Ministry" recognizes that ordained ministers have unique roles in the life of the church as those who are called to be "zealous in maintaining both the truth of the gospel and the peace of the church, . . . faithful in preaching and teaching the gospel, in administering the sacraments and rites of the church, and in exercising pastoral care and leadership."[7]

Though pastors have unique gifts within the body of Christ, they share their gifts in a democracy of revelation, inspiration, and vocation. As I stated earlier in the chapter, God inspires and works through every member of the body. Pastors do not minister to a godless world or a church bereft of inspiration, despite the brokenness of our world. Rather, everyone they encounter has been touched by God and lives and moves and has their being (Acts 17:28) in a world in which divine grace and inspiration are universal. As Paul aptly says in 1 Corinthians 12, pastors have gifts, but so does everyone else in the congregation; pastors are inspired, but so are children, senior adults, single people, parents, and youth. No one is excluded from God's vocational call. As Paul affirms, "Now there are varieties of gifts, but the same Spirit; and there are varieties of services, but the same Lord; and there are varieties of activities, but it is the same God who activates all of them in everyone. To each is given the manifestation of the Spirit for the common good" (1 Cor. 12:4–7).

One primary expression of pastoral authority is awakening the sense of God's presence throughout the congregation. Years ago, I heard the celebrated pastor and preaching professor Ernie Campbell say, "There are only two kinds of people in the world, those who are in God's hands and know it, and those who are in God's hands and don't." I believe that the same could be said for the nature of divine inspiration: "There are only two kinds of people in the world, those who are inspired by God and know it, and those who are inspired by God and have yet to realize it." Each person within the church, including the pastor, has a vocation—or perhaps many vocations, in the spirit of John Calvin and Martin Luther, in multiple arenas—in service of God and the world, and the pastor's call is to awaken people and communities to their own unique callings.

Just as pastors experience the call to ministry and have been touched by God, lay people also experience God's ever-present and ongoing inspiration in their lives. God relates personally and intimately to all of us, bringing forth our gifts within our particular life experience and context. Still, within the body of Christ, the ongoing call to ministry and the nature of pastoral authority is always evolving because of new challenges in the community and new guidance from God.

With ministerial authority comes power to shape congregational life. As Jackson Carroll asserts, "To exercise authority involves influencing, directing, coordinating, or otherwise guiding the thoughts and behaviors of people and groups in ways that they consider legitimate."[8] The question for pastors as they seek to use their authority in wise ways is, How shall we use the power invested in us by our personal and institutional call and ordination? How can we use our power to encourage laypeople to claim their vocation and live out God's vision for the church and all creation?

In describing the nature of power, whether personal or professional, one of my professors, Bernard Loomer, spoke of two kinds of power: relational and coercive power.[9] Coercive power is unilateral and seeks to influence others without taking their own gifts seriously. Pastors who use coercive power, even if they feel they are guided by God, lead but do not listen and are unwilling to alter their vision in response to the congregation's gifts and needs. In contrast, relational power is grounded in authentic mutuality and respect for the experience and value of others. It recognizes that authority is always relational and grounded in our openness to embrace the gifts and experiences of others. In the spirit of 1 Corinthians 12, the pastor's unique gifts and calling, affirmed by ordination, serve God's vision of vitality and health for the congregation to which he or she is called. Such power is visionary and persuasive rather than domineering. Taking inspiration from Jesus's words to his followers in John 14:12—"The one who believes in me will also do the works that I do and, in fact, will do greater works than these"—the relational pastor seeks to maximize the congregation's use of freedom and power for creative purposes. Leadership, therefore, is a form of service in which pastors are called to cast a *vision* of church and its mission, but not an *agenda*, an inflexible attitude toward achieving the pastor's particular vision. They are vision inspired rather than purpose driven, trusting that God's vision and movements will unfold in the dynamic movements of call and response, rather than by the pastor's force of will. They recognize that the church is a laboratory for spiritual formation, visionary thinking, and missional action, and that their goal is to nurture the awareness of God's unfolding call at every level of congregational life. In the spirit of Celia Hahn's image of integrated authority, they claim their vocation as serving the well-being of the whole by supporting the vocations of others in the body of Christ.

Life-Giving Authority

Authority in the church is life-giving for both pastor and congregants when it is relational, grounded in the mutual commitment of congregation and pastor to support one another through prayer, listening, and common vision. Relationship does not require uniformity but common respect and willingness to bear one another's burdens and affirm one another's gifts and insights. Authority and the power that goes with it are intended for the health of the whole, not the realization of the pastor's vision. As one pastor notes, "Once I got to know them and they got to know me, we were able to move forward in mission. It took awhile, but once they saw my gifts, experienced my care, and trusted my commitment to them, they took my leadership seriously."

Second, life-giving authority is spiritual, grounded in the pastor's commitment to deepening her or his spiritual life. As Chris stated above, her authority is rooted in being a nonanxious presence in times of congregational change. Becoming a nonanxious presence is the result of a pastor's commitment to joining her or his spiritual practices with awareness of congregational family systems. In addition, the nonanxious and spiritually grounded pastor seeks to be mindful of the way he or she responds to others, especially in stressful situations. Healthy authority recognizes the reality of resistance but responds to resistance through differentiated care and nondefensiveness. The reality of resistance challenges pastors to develop their spiritual lives and to trust that in all things, nothing "will be able to separate us from the love of God in Christ Jesus our Lord" (Rom. 8:39).

Third, life-giving authority is differentiated. The pastor is in but not of the congregation because of both call and ordination. Differentiation joined with care-full intimacy is essential to healthy leadership. According to Peter Steinke, leaders are the congregation's "stewards, people who are willing to be accountable for the welfare of the system . . . [in order to] keep the system's direction aligned with its purpose."[10] Differentiated leadership is characterized by "calm, reflective, and principle-based action."[11] By having a flexible definition of their role, pastors become agents of change and stewards of the congregational call. By staying in touch with their congregation's experiences and values, pastors are able to use the resources of the congregation to promote health, vitality, and mission. They can speak the truth with love and fidelity.

Fourth, life-giving authority in ministry is visionary, grounded in the pastor's imaginative openness to God's vision for the church and the world. Like her or his congregants, the pastor needs to be open to God's surprising alternatives. God is always doing a new thing, and this may call even the most creative and visionary pastor beyond her or his comfort zone. The visionary pastor recognizes that God is working throughout the congregation and not only through her or his ministerial imagination and skills. Constantly cultivating what Craig Dykstra describes as the pastoral imagination, visionary pastors look for surprises and God-moments and assume that their congregants are also experiencing God's call forward, even if congregants are unaware of it or resist it. The visionary pastor begins with her or his own imagination but seeks to cultivate a community of vision and mission in which old and young alike dream dreams and see visions.

Fifth, life-giving authority in ministry uses power in ways that nurture greater faithfulness, creativity, and freedom among congregants. Liberated from zero-sum, scarcity-oriented approaches to power, pastors claim their own responsibility to shape and influence congregational life, while allowing themselves to be influenced by others. They see their vision as a fluid process rather than a fixed destination. Like the magi who visited Jesus's family, the visionary pastor realizes that in the dynamic interplay of divine call and human response, the congregation and the pastor may have to travel "by another road" from what they initially thought (Matt. 2:12).

Creative Wisdom for Healthy Authority

Healthy pastoral authority is grounded in our vision of the body of Christ and our vocation as pastors within it. I invite you, first, to take some time to read meditatively the words of 1 Corinthians 12:12–31, noting in the spirit of *lectio divina* any words, images, or phrases that emerge from your reading. Reflect on what they mean for your current ministerial setting. Where are you experiencing gifts within your congregation? What gifts are being brought forth in your own life? To ground this exercise, take some time to pray for the gifts that you notice and send a message (through e-mail, letter, or Facebook) of thanks to those people whose gifts you identify.

Later this week, take some time to read 1 Corinthians 12:12–31 again in preparation for practicing the following imaginative prayer or contemplative visualization. As you enter this time of holy imagination, I invite you to take some time simply to center yourself quietly, noticing your breath, inhaling and exhaling. When you experience a peaceful state, begin this imaginative prayer by visualizing a healthy, vital, lively body of whatever size or shape comes to mind. Visualize its external health and well-being. Now, take a moment to look deeper, beneath the surface, and imagine the creative interdependence of the various bodily parts in supporting one another. Visualize how each one depends on the healthy functioning of its companions in the body.

Using your imagination, consider the part of the body that represents your contribution to the whole organism. What are your particular gifts? What do you need to be healthy?

Now step back a moment, letting your image of a healthy body blur into the body of Christ, manifested by the congregation you are currently serving. As you imaginatively consider this body, how would you describe its overall health and well-being? Looking deeper and without judgment, notice the parts of the body that are functioning in a healthy fashion and those that are currently diseased. Notice how they affect the well-being of the whole.

Pause a moment to visualize your own role in the body of Christ, manifested by your congregation. What are your gifts to the overall body? How would you describe your overall well-being within the body? What other "organs" support your well-being within the congregation? What do you need to be healthier in your role as leader within the body? What new visions lie ahead for you in order to fulfill your vocation in the body?

Conclude again with a time of stillness. Take some time to write in your journal about your experience. Perhaps this exercise will challenge you to take new initiatives in your vocation, to ask for help within or beyond the congregation, or to reach out to parts of the body in need of greater care or healing. If there are people to whom you need to express gratitude, take time to thank to them.

CHAPTER 4

WHEN THE HONEYMOON'S OVER, IF THERE EVER WAS ONE

All spoke well of [Jesus] and were amazed at the gracious words that came from his mouth. . . . When they heard [Jesus's message], all in the synagogue were filled with rage. They got up, drove him out of the town, and led him to the brow of the hill on which their town was built, so that they might hurl him off the cliff. But he passed through the midst of them and went on his way.

—LUKE 4:22, 28–30

The Honeymoon as a Time of Growth

In ministry, many new pastors discover how quickly the tide turns and the "perfect" congregation becomes a problem child. As I ponder issues of conflict and resistance in ministry, I must first make the confession that I am a fan of Hallmark and Lifetime movies. I like happy endings and enjoy seeing these stories of couples who finally come together, despite the obstacles, and look forward to living happily ever after. But often after I turn off the movie, I realize that the work of relationships just begins with falling in love. As one who has been married more than thirty years, I have lived through several "mini-marriages," seasons of joy, alienation, challenge, comfort, and expectation. I expect a few more in the decades ahead! I must admit that I love being married and rejoice in life with my wife, Kate. But I must also confess that marriage isn't always easy, as two unique and contrasting personalities, with differing family histories and ideas about recreation and personal priorities, try to make a healthy and loving home together.

More than one pastor has, for good or bad reasons, compared ministry to a long-term marital partnership. It begins with the first glance, often revealed when a pastor drives by a congregation that is looking for a pastor or reads the congregational profile and decides that there might be a fit between her or his gifts and their needs. Next comes the courtship of e-mails, phone calls, and arranged meetings. The initial relationship often has a degree of secrecy, a circle of confidentiality (often more like a sieve) involving the potential candidate and her or his future congregation. "Dates," phone calls, and meetings with the search committee and the neutral pulpit precede coming to meet the family—that is, the congregation—for the candidating, or trial, sermon, and finally the engagement and the ceremony of installation, making tangible the spiritual covenant that already exists. Everyone has great hopes for transformation and new life; eventually, there are a few disappointments, even in the healthiest relationships and ministries. Even the United Methodist Church's appointment process involves first meetings, hopeful beginnings, and the hard work of creating a healthy partnership in ministry. Healthy and growing pastor-congregation relationships, like intimate relational partnerships, require a good deal of grace, serendipity, vision, and intentionality if they are to flourish over the long haul.

Lyn, the pastor of a United Church of Christ congregation in Lititz, Pennsylvania, shared her insights on her pastoral honeymoon as we drank hot cocoa at the Cafe Chocolate, near the famous Wilbur's Chocolate Factory in Lititz. Lyn noted that, for her, "the point of the honeymoon is to use that special time to build relationships, discover how the church works, and become familiar with the congregation's leadership." The honeymoon is a time when the pastor and congregation see the best in each other and can take time to get to know each other "so that when the honeymoon's over, it's not a problem. We can deal with the tough issues because we've built a relational foundation during the honeymoon." To my surprise, Lyn affirmed that "when the honeymoon's over, the fun begins. We can be honest and then get to work as partners in the church's mission."

Karen, a Mennonite pastor in suburban Lancaster, Pennsylvania, saw her honeymoon as a time of joy that still remains. "While they received me with open arms as their first female pastor, I felt amazement and joy that I was in the role of a pastor. As a Mennonite woman, I couldn't believe that it would happen, but it did!" Like Lyn, Karen built good relationships during the honeymoon period that have allowed her ministry to mature. Karen notices that she experienced an inner change that alerted her that the honeymoon was over. As she reflects, "I felt a change in myself. While the euphoria of being a pastor has diminished, I still feel tremendous joy. I can be with them as we go through difficult things. It's a riper kind of joy. Now that the honeymoon's over, we can go deeper. I see people growing in faith and in congregational life together."

Jonathan, a United Church of Christ pastor in the Philadelphia suburbs, feels fortunate at the positive experience he has had in the six years of his first congregational call and is looking forward to a long pastorate at this congregation. About eighteen months into his call, Jonathan remembers telling his congregation's pastoral relations committee that he still felt like they were in the honeymoon experience. Although they responded with the judgment "It's over," neither Jonathan nor the congregation leaders saw that as a problem. Both the committee and Jonathan affirmed the overall health of the congregation and positive feelings toward his pastoral leadership. In many ways, Jonathan attributes his very fortunate circumstances to the problem-solving of the interim pastor, who dealt directly with a number of issues that had led to conflicts within the congregation and with previous pastors. Jonathan gratefully acknowledges, "When I got there, they were ready to move forward. Some of the divisive members had left, and the church was ready to make a new start with a new pastor." The overall health of Jonathan's congregation has enabled him to grow steadily in ministry without feelings of defensiveness or challenge from the outside. Although he admits to "being my own worst critic," Jonathan recognizes that "in my sixth year in ministry, I feel like I've barely started, and I still have a lot to learn, especially about leadership. As an introvert, I often listen before I respond and am now learning to experiment with leadership in the context of a very healthy situation."

Now in her fourth month at a new call, Monica, who spent four years as an associate pastor, rejoices in her current honeymoon experience. "Everything I do is OK—even when I try something new in church." Like Jonathan, Monica is grateful for the sensitivity and skill of an interim pastor. According to Monica, "This was a congregation that had some conflict in the past and needed to heal. The interim tackled the conflict issues, worked through feelings of anger and hurt, taught them about worship, and helped them develop policies related to congregational procedures and relationships." Monica adds, "There is still pain from the past, but there has been a lot of healing. I am blessed to be here and to be part of a congregation that is growing in attendance, recovering its vision, and worshiping with joy."

Sarah, a United Church of Christ pastor in a congregation outside of York, Pennsylvania, notes, "I can't tell if I'm on a honeymoon after my first six months in ministry." She adds:

When I came to this rural congregation, they were very friendly, but I realize that they had to deal with some issues that were new to them. I was their first female pastor, and I was also the youngest pastor, only twenty-eight, that they had called. I recall one leader exclaiming, "Oh my gosh, you're so young." Still, I think their willingness to be flexible brought out my own flexibility, especially in worship leadership. I didn't initially intend to change anything, but it happened organically.

Like Jonathan, Monica, and a number of other new pastors with whom I spoke, Sarah has high praise for the role of a competent interim minister. In her case, the interim helped the congregation explore new and more flexible forms of worship, which paved the way for Sarah's more informal and contemporary approach to worship.

Now in her sixth year at a suburban Pittsburgh, Pennsylvania, Disciples of Christ congregation, Jana, reflects, "I definitely had a honeymoon. At the beginning, I was more energetic, filled with possibilities. It was like an unopened present, what the congregation and I could do together." In remembering her honeymoon period in ministry, Jana recalls, "It's a lot like a courtship. At first you're wooing each other, putting your best foot forward, wanting to be liked." But, then the challenges of real ministry with real people come. As Jana confesses, "The shift comes when we get back to reality, when the illusion is over and the magic didn't happen. In the honeymoon period, the congregation is under the illusion that you, as the pastor, can grow the church and fix their problems all by yourself. But when they realize that you can't perform a miracle, then the congregation feels let down." Jana notes that pastors also bring their own illusions to a new congregation: "I expected more of some of the spiritual leaders, who initially impressed me by their spiritual maturity; it was hard when some of these people didn't want to walk the talk of spiritual growth."

The honeymoon period provides a type of moratorium that allows the pastor to explore new things with the congregation, although sometimes novelty is met with resistance. When Jana introduced the idea of Christian practices, as popularized by Dorothy Bass and Diana Butler Bass,[1] she expected the church leadership to get on board, but "I was met with resistance by the people that I perceived to be most spiritual when I introduced healing and prayer practices. I was disappointed that they didn't want to grow."

Jana used much of her honeymoon time for spiritual and professional growth and wanted to bring her insights back to the congregation. In words reminiscent of a marital relationship in which a couple grows apart when one member returns to school, Jana notes, "I started to change and grow, and was learning new things about congregational spirituality, and wanted to share my growth with them. But they didn't appreciate my new ideas. Then, I knew for sure that the honeymoon was over, on both sides. The shine came off, and I had to do the hard work of ministry as an imperfect pastor working with imperfect people."

Although the honeymoon was over and she received a lot of push-back from her congregation, Jana stayed connected with her "imperfect" congregation. Now in her sixth year at the church, she attributes her staying power to her willingness to focus on the congregation's gifts and forward movement rather than its problems. Jana says, "We are getting closer to having mission at the heart of what we do." Jana's commitment to seeing the church from a larger perspective is also evident in her longevity in ministry: "The longer ministry I have here, the healthier their ministry will be. I want to be here long enough to help them work through some of the problems I inherited as well as some unresolved issues that emerged when the honeymoon ended." For Jana, pastoral leadership is a covenantal relationship that challenges the pastor to faithful presence and companionship, even when her or his ideas meet strong resistance.

At this point, I must add that some congregational situations are toxic for new pastors. Wounds haven't healed or a foundation for trusting pastoral leadership hasn't been laid. In some cases, socially alienating or dysfunctional behaviors are tolerated to the point that a pastor must move on in order to preserve her or his own health and ministerial vocation. In other cases, pastor and congregation simply do not fit together in a creative partnership; for one reason or another, their unique gifts don't match. Although no acrimony may be present, eventually pastor and congregation must choose to part, moving on with each other's blessing.

Ruthann, a United Church of Christ pastor who left her Central Pennsylvania congregation, laments that her congregation chose not to call an interim before she began her pastorate: "I didn't have a honeymoon because there was no one to pave the way and heal the wounds that this congregation had experienced in the past. It was a hurt congregation that wasn't given the chance to heal. An interim would have given them an opportunity to go through a healing process, deal with conflict, look at strengths and limitations, and plan for the future."

Chris, a Central Pennsylvania Presbyterian pastor, appreciated the grace she experienced on her pastoral honeymoon. According to Chris, "It's a time to explore and discover the church's challenges as well as growing edges. I pushed a few boundaries at the church, first, by moving the baptismal font from the back of the church to beside the chancel as a theological reminder of the centrality of baptism in Christian life." Chris says that while she received a few comments about moving the font, she received more push-back when she decided to move the flag from the chancel to a room adjacent to the sanctuary. As Chris recalls, "I took the flag out the first Advent I was there, and while they initially didn't make any comments, they asked, 'When are you bringing it back?'" I brought it back for several weeks, and then took it out of the sanctuary during Lent. I felt it was important for them to remember what they truly worship, God or the flag."

Chris admits that the exploration works both ways. "They are getting to know you as you get to know them. The honeymoon is a time of building trust; without mutual trust, you can't move forward in ministry." Chris discovered that her goal of being a nonanxious presence was helpful during times of resistance. One key element that Chris noticed and then addressed during her honeymoon was the general attitude that "you don't rock the boat at church. Folks would rather avoid dealing with conflict than addressing it. But, if you don't risk rocking the boat, there's no way to have honest communication." In building a sense of trust, Chris was able to address the church's challenges directly. As she notes, "Now we just talk about issues rather than avoid them." Together, Chris and her congregation are learning that direct communication is essential to healing, both personal and congregational.

Paul, a Disciples of Christ pastor from Oklahoma, resonates with the story of the response of Jesus's hometown to his first sermon. He reflects:

> I came to the church right out of seminary in my midtwenties. I was so young, and they cut me some slack as I matured as a leader. But, when I actually became a leader and claimed my authority in the church, they initially pushed back hard. When they realized that I had matured in ministry and could respond to their resistance, they began to take me seriously, pushing back but also letting me guide them. I became a grown-up in their eyes and had earned their respect.

Paul survived the end of his pastoral honeymoon by facing the resistance without defensiveness. He was willing to grow along with his congregation, flexibly responding to them while maintaining his own vision of ministerial leadership.

Jennifer, a United Church of Christ pastor of a town-and-country church in Westminster, Maryland, remembers that when she began, "I felt like it was a honeymoon. They gave me and my husband lots of gifts, especially food, that first Christmas. Each year, the gifts dwindled, which to me was a sign that the honeymoon was over." Her congregation had a history of scapegoating its pastors, many of whom left after only a few years. Jennifer admits that about three years into her ministry, this scapegoating began to occur with her as well. Now in her sixth year, Jennifer recalls:

> What helped me deal with the grumbling and gossip was the great support from other clergy, Lancaster Theological Seminary's program for new pastors, and a competent and supportive judicatory official. I responded prayerfully and lovingly, but in dealing with some difficult situations, I stood firm. I gathered the Pastoral Relations Committee and other church leaders and told them what I had been observing. While it was difficult for them to challenge unhealthy behaviors in the church, they came through.

Jennifer attributes her positive response to congregational problems to three choices she made: she reached out to trusted, experienced pastors and the area conference minister; communicated clearly and engaged in mutual give and take with congregants, including congregational leaders; and paid attention to her spiritual life. As Jennifer recollects, "I did my inner work. I worked hard at practicing nonviolence in my thoughts and actions. It would have been easy to feel defensive. But I did the hard work of looking beyond their behaviors to see God's presence in congregants, even when I had to speak frankly with them about problematic behaviors." Jennifer adds that she was able to respond more clearly and peacefully as a result of a two-day workshop she attended, "Anxiety and the Church." Studying family and congregational systems at the workshop helped Jennifer "differentiate herself from the congregation and note what she was passionate about and where she needed to stand her ground." At a congregational annual meeting some time later, a church leader noted appreciatively and humorously that as a result of clear and differentiated communication, "we learned where she wasn't going to budge, and we both learned where we weren't going to budge." Directness between Jennifer and her congregation has created a synergetic environment where new and creative things are happening, and where the congregation is enjoying the benefits of stable pastoral leadership.

When the Honeymoon's Over

I often tell new pastors that ministry is a marathon, not a sprint. Faithful excellence in ministry is grounded in taking advantage of the honeymoon period and not panicking when the honeymoon is over. Most of the pastors with whom I have spoken see the honeymoon period, first, as a time for building relationships and trust with congregants. The relationship-building time is also a time for exploration. Like the TV detective Colombo, the new pastor can pretend to be the dumbest person in the room, innocently asking probing questions that will help identify the congregation's challenges as well as its possibilities. Many pastors use the honeymoon as a time for experimentation and making small changes that may lead over time to profound congregational transformation.

When the honeymoon is over and the pastor notices resistance among congregants, he or she is tempted to succumb to self-doubt, anxiety, or feelings of alienation. The most effective new pastors see this period of mutual disillusionment and congregational resistance as an opportunity for spiritual and professional growth.[2] Some new pastors, like Jennifer, focus on spiritual growth, withdraw projections, and learn to see holiness in the most challenging people. The philosopher Alfred North Whitehead observed that within the limitations we face, new opportunities may emerge. This affirmation is true for congregations as well as people. While this does not ensure an easy transition, pastors who look for possibilities amid challenges tend to be more patient with their congregation's imperfections. Again, patience is essential here. As Lyn and Karen state, when the euphoria is over, the good work of ministry can continue and deepen.

During times of transition, pastors find inner resources by focusing on their spiritual lives. In the spirit of psychiatrist Victor Frankl, who wrote of his experiences in a Nazi concentration camp, while pastors can't control others' behaviors and responses, they can be responsible for their own attitudes. Becoming a nonanxious presence is the result of a pastor cultivating spiritual disciplines that enable him or her to weather the storms of ministry, face challenges, and grow in ministerial wisdom and stature. Chris and Jennifer found that learning about the dynamics of congregational systems freed them from the burdens of self-blame and self-doubt and allowed them to claim their own leadership styles and communicate directly in ways that nurtured partnership rather than alienation.

When the honeymoon is over, both pastors and congregations may find that they see their church—its relational dynamics, decision-making processes, and limitations—in a new light. While this can lead to disillusionment, it may also deepen the covenantal love between a pastor and her or his congregation. In Jennifer's case, she chose the pathway of appreciation, of seeing their gifts and looking for God's presence disguised in each congregant. Her own commitment to see God in her congregants enabled her to communicate in loving and direct ways. When pastors remember that everyone we meet is bearing a burden, our empathy can lead to positive ministry, even if behaviors or circumstances do not immediately change.

Many pastors note that when they discover that the honeymoon's over, they need to reach out to people beyond the congregation. Healthy professional relationships and mentoring enable us to let go of our own illusions, discern what is really going on in the congregation, and discover appropriate and creative responses to congregational challenges and resistance. The insights of experienced pastors who've "been there" or who have no emotional stake in the congregational dynamics enable a new pastor to gain new perspective on her or his work and the congregation's gifts and challenges.

Creative Wisdom When the Honeymoon's Over

Healthy ministry involves practicing the presence of God in the many seasons and tasks of ministry.[3] Most of us are inclined to believe that stress and resistance provide few opportunities for spiritual growth. While we may wish to avoid challenging times in ministry, God is as present in moments of conflict as in moments of harmony. Recognizing God's presence in the challenges of ministry involves a combination of God's grace and the minister's openness. While I don't wish to minimize the challenges that occur when the honeymoon is over, I invite you to consider the following exercises as ways of building creative relationships over the long haul and enabling you to embody the best practices of new pastors described in this chapter. Remember that while you can't necessarily change others' behaviors or the congregational environment, you can seek to have a transformed mind and new vision (Rom. 12:2).

Begin with some deep breathing, simply to center yourself and place yourself in God's presence. After a few minutes, visualize your congregation as realistically as possible, opening to the limitations and possibilities, conflicts and achievements of the congregation. Take a moment to prayerfully surround each congregational situation as it emerges in God's loving light. Notice the holiness, deep down, in people who are challenging or difficult. Experience their deeper reality as God's beloved children. See yourself responding creatively to them in ways that honor your vocation and well-being as well as their behaviors and deepest needs. Close with a prayer for the well-being of the church and its mission in the community.

Often when pastors experience conflict in their congregations, old fears emerge as we feel vulnerable personally and professionally. In the Celtic tradition, whenever a person leaves on a journey, he or she draws a circle around him- or herself. This encircling exercise, or *caim*, was seen as both a source of protection and a reminder that God surrounds us every step of the journey. God is behind, in front of, above, beneath, encircling us in ways that inspire and protect. If you are in a public place and cannot physically move, you can draw an imaginary circle around yourself whenever you feel at risk.

A third practice for new pastors involves becoming aware that your very presence injects new possibilities into the congregation's life. In addition, the novelty of a new congregation opens the new pastor to surprise, possibility, and adventure. Although I don't suggest making radical changes in the congregation initially unless they are called for or you receive divine guidance, your awareness that, noticed or unnoticed, change is occurring is liberating. Change often leads to resistance, which is not necessarily bad, but reflects the desire to preserve familiar traditions and rituals of the congregation. Awareness of the realities of change and resistance allows you to gently make changes that honor life-giving traditions in your congregation. In this context, take some time to imagine and reflect on what changes are occurring in you as a pastor and person. In a corresponding way, consider what changes are emerging within the congregation simply because you—and not someone else— have been called to be their pastor. What new energy or unexpected resistance have your unique gifts, style, and personality brought forth? This resistance and energy can be perceived as positive, since novelty may inspire, console, or agitate. Take time to pray for creative ways to use your gifts in this time of congregational change.

CHAPTER 5

BOUNDARIES THAT HEAL PASTORS AND CONGREGATIONS

In the morning, while it was still very dark, [Jesus] got up and went out to a deserted place, and there he prayed. And Simon and his companions hunted for him. When they found him, they said to him, "Everyone is searching for you." He answered, "Let us go on to the neighboring towns, so that I may proclaim the message there also; for that is what I came out to do."

—MARK 1:35–38

RECENTLY, I USED THIS PASSAGE AS THE BASIS FOR A TIME OF *lectio divina* with group of new pastors. Many of them heard these words as if for the first time. One pastor responded, "Jesus needed to pray. How is that possible?" Another chimed in, "Jesus needed to get away. I wish that I had his discipline and created places for prayer and rest in my ministry." A third added, "I noticed that the disciples went looking for Jesus. That sounds like my church. They want good sermons, but the schedule is so crazy, I don't get much time for preparation." To which a fourth responded, "Jesus was busy, too, but he took time for prayer. He chose to be alone."

Now, issues of boundaries are challenging and often mis-understood in ministry. On the one hand, every rural pastor has heard a story like Steve's: "One morning, I came down for breakfast, with just shorts on, to discover three trustees in the kitchen, measuring the length of the room in preparation for some parsonage improvements. Thank goodness my wife was still in bed!" On the other extreme are stories I hear from lay-people about pastors who say, "It's my day off, and I won't go to the emergency room," or "I want comp time whenever I work over forty hours a week." (I must note that no new pastor has confessed to such a statement.)

Yes, boundaries in ministry are challenging and often mis-understood by both clergy and laity. Faith, who serves a United Methodist congregation on the Chesapeake Bay in Maryland, aptly states, "Issues of boundaries are blurry in ministry. We are granted access into other people's lives, we know some of their deepest secrets, and often they expect the same access into [our lives.]" Historically, pastors belong to the one of the three professional traditions—law, medicine, and priesthood—but are accessible to their congregants in ways that would be rare in law and medicine. As Faith notes, "Doctors also have access to folks' lives, but you wouldn't expect to hear intimate details about your doctor's life or to stop over at his or her house un-announced." Tony, the pastor of a German Reformed United Church congregation in Western Pennsylvania, confesses, "In small towns, your life is always on display, and you're always being watched. It's hard to find time just to be myself." Bound-aries in ministry are grounded in the maturity, character, and integrity of pastors in partnership with their congregations. Tony notes that when pastor and community get to know one another and share a common mission, the congregation begins to accept its role as partner in ministry rather than spectator in relationship to the new minister. Boundaries are, first, matters of intention and integrity and, then, matters of relationship and behavior.

The Nature of Boundaries

Boundaries are essential to healthy living. In fact, boundaries are built into the nature of reality. On the one hand, we are profoundly relational beings, shaped by our families of origin, the environment, our current relationships, and most recent encounters. On the other hand, each of us needs solitude, even if only the solitude of our thoughts and emotions at certain times, to grow and flourish. Whether in community or congregational life, the midseventeenth-century proverb popularized by Robert Frost makes good sense: "Good fences make good neighbors." Healthy boundaries define who we are and what we need to flourish without alienating our neighbors or congregants.

Because ministry is relational in nature, creative and flexible boundaries are essential to healthy ministry for the vocational and personal well-being of both the pastor and her or his congregants. A pastor who is too aloof and doesn't connect with her or his congregants cannot fully minister to the people or guide them in charting their congregational vision. But a pastor who is too connected and is "one of us" loses her or his prophetic integrity in ministry and unintentionally intrudes on congregants' privacy in ways that are unhealthy for the congregation and the pastor. Still, how pastors live out creative boundaries is contextual and reflects the history of the congregation's relationships with its previous pastors, its current needs, and the congregation's culture. In rural churches, congregants typically expect pastors to make home visits and the pastor regularly receives gifts of produce to help feed her or his family and supplement his or her modest income. The pastor who refuses such generosity may forfeit the intimacy necessary for good rural ministry. In contrast to their rural colleagues, suburban and urban pastors rarely do home visits and tend to meet people at the church or neutral places such as coffeehouses or restaurants.

In the interdependent world of congregational life, pastors need to be creatively differentiated in every aspect of ministry and personal life. They need to embody in a flexible way the spiritual integrity, appropriate self-disclosure, personal privacy, and respectful behavior that set them apart from others, able to challenge congregational values and behaviors. They also need to be appropriately transparent, connected, and sympathetic with their congregants. In actuality, healthy behavioral boundaries are intimately connected with pastoral self-care and mindfulness. As social worker and massage therapist Nina McIntosh notes, "Boundaries are like protective circles surrounding the professional relationship."[1] Pastors who have no personal boundaries, who do not flexibly differentiate their lives from their parishioners, are more likely to intrude inappropriately in the lives of their congregants. For relationships to be healthy, pastoral boundaries need to define the appropriate degree of self-disclosure and personal sharing; to reflect the realities of trauma, abuse, and sexual misconduct and harassment (even) in the church; and to allow sacred space for congregants' spiritual, emotional, and physical lives.

Before turning to the words of new pastors on healthy and flexible boundary keeping, I want to explore the complexity of ministerial-leadership boundaries. First, boundaries are essential to ministerial self-affirmation and the fulfillment of the pastor's vocation. In the passage from Mark's Gospel quoted at the beginning of this chapter, Jesus goes to a solitary place and intentionally separates himself from his community in order to find spiritual refreshment. Jesus needs distance from the crowds in order to fulfill his mission and appropriately respond to people's needs.

Second, boundaries enable pastors to professionally differentiate ourselves from our parishioners while welcoming them into our lives. In Mark's Gospel, the disciples "hunted" for Jesus, intruding upon his prayer time. Even though they are no doubt anxious, they triangulate the situation, claiming, "Everyone is searching for you." Faithful excellence in ministry requires pastors to know their communities' boundaries and adapt to them, while affirming their own need for prayer, professional distance, prophetic integrity, and privacy. As I noted earlier, boundaries are related to community mores. For example, few pastors of metropolitan or suburban congregations encounter their congregants in the course of dinner out with their spouse or partner, nor would they expect a parishioner to stop by their home unannounced. In contrast, small town pastors encounter their congregants at the grocery store, elementary school, movie theater (if there is one!), and local restaurants. This built-in intimacy led one pastor to exclaim, "I can't get away from them at all. They're mowing the parsonage lawn next door to the church and waving at me, wanting me to stop in when I'm trying to work on my sermon. I feel suffocated." As a result of good counsel by another small town pastor, he now visits friends on his day off, goes to the library to study, and makes plans to go away for an overnight in the city at least once a month.

Third, solid but flexible boundaries enable us to appropriately enter others' lives and maintain confidentiality. While my intent is not to focus directly on pastoral misconduct, virtually every pastor recalls a time in which he or she said too much about a congregant or had to be mindful about becoming too intimate with a congregant or church family. Good personal and professional boundaries are health giving as well as preventive; they keep us professionally and personally healthy and out of trouble as pastors, on the one hand, and enable us to claim our vocation as pastors, teachers, and prophets on the other.

Fourth, good boundaries are grounded in a sense of personal mission and vocation. In Mark's Gospel, Jesus is able to gently say no to his disciples and the crowd when they want him to settle in one place, because he is clear about his vision and vocation. Jesus's boundary-keeping behavior is summarized in his response: "Let us go on to the neighboring towns, so that I may proclaim the message there also; for that is what I came out to do" (Mark 1:38).

Finally, the words of Mark 6:14–46 suggest that awareness of boundaries helps us maintain an intimate relationship between spirituality, self-care, and pastoral compassion. After hearing of John the Baptist's death and welcoming his disciples back from their successful preaching tour, Jesus goes on a brief retreat with them. Although it appears that the retreat is cut short by the needs of the crowd, Jesus, rather than being annoyed, has compassion on them and is able to feed them both spiritually and physically. Jesus's approach to professional ministry is a far cry from that reflected in the comment made by a young pastor several years ago: "This matter of self-care is sheer narcissism; as pastors our lives are poured out for others in self-sacrifice. We must be willing to go to the cross for God's glory." While I appreciate his commitment and theology of sacrifice, I responded by reminding him that just as Jesus prayed and rested so that he could care for others, pastors must be nourished by a spiritual wellspring to be effective in ministry. Healthy boundaries create a circle of care that embraces both pastor and congregants alike. They announce to every congregant that their contacts with their pastor will be safe, life-giving, confidential, and healing in nature.

Ruthann, a Central Pennsylvania United Church of Christ pastor, sees boundaries as emerging from a pastor's calling. She believes, "Boundaries are not just a mandate from the judicatories but also grounded in God's calling, and that's for a whole lifetime. Our calling is the primary element in boundary keeping. Because God calls us to ministry, we maintain a higher degree of self-awareness, self-sacrifice, and commitment. My calling to ministry shapes every aspect of my life, from my personal values to my care for my congregation."

Brian, a United Methodist pastor from Northern Virginia, agrees: "Boundaries are a matter of call and character. I am serving God in all I do, and this means putting my congregants and the congregation first. The call to ministry is to equip the saints and not satisfy my own needs."

In my Lancaster Theological Seminary course "Transitions to Ministry," we ponder the relationship of boundaries to professional life. One participant asserted, "To be a professional is to believe something and then act on it. If I believe that God calls me to be a pastor, caring for my flock, my primary responsibility is to truly care for them." Another participant stated, "It's about God and not me; my calling is to be a healer, and that requires me to seek healing in every pastoral encounter." Still another said, "Sometimes the boundary training is frightening. It puts us on the defensive as pastors, assuming that we're going to do something wrong or that a parishioner might make a false accusation. For me, it's about healthy ministry—about caring for myself so that I can care for others; about knowing myself so that I can respond to others; and behaving myself so that others will be benefited."

But, as Faith commented, "boundaries are blurry" and require pastors to be self-aware, flexible, and differentiated in their congregational leadership and relationships.

Finding the Golden Mean in Boundary Keeping

As I have already stated, creative boundary keeping in ministry begins with the affirmation that the concern is for congregants as well as pastors. In fact, while we pastors always minister as people who have our own needs, histories, preferences, and visions, our goal is ultimately the well-being of our congregants and the well-being of the church shaped by God's vision of shalom and wholeness. Still, as the apostle Paul notes in 1 Corinthians 13, we see in a mirror dimly. Recognizing the limitations of our own understanding and self-awareness is essential to healthy and affirming ministry. We never fully know what is best for the congregant who seeks our pastoral guidance or the full details of God's vision for our congregation. What this means in the concrete practices of relational ministry is that we exercise our professional boundaries with great care and empathy, neither too little nor too much. For example, in an earlier chapter I shared the story of the congregant who innocently said to one new pastor, "I'm sure glad we're friends," the pastor's immediate reply, "I can't be your friend, I'm your pastor," led to awkward silence and a hasty physical and emotional withdrawal by the congregant, which took weeks to mend. While the pastor's remark represented, in the abstract, good professional advice, the delivery was harmful to her relationship with her congregant and no doubt was experienced as a put-down by the congregant, who intended her comment to communicate the affection she had for her pastor and not to intrude on her professional vocation. As I noted earlier, in retrospect, this pastor confessed, "I wish I'd been a little more subtle. I could have said something like, 'Please remember that, first of all, I'm your pastor, and because I'm your pastor, you can count on me to care for you even if we don't always get along.'"

How we practice pastoral boundaries is important in that dynamic interplay of differentiation and connection, especially since few congregants have boundary training and many will relate to their pastor according to familiar behavior patterns, learned as young children in their family of origin. They often assume an intimacy that is not shared by their pastor. This, of course, is understandable, since many congregants bare their souls to their pastor and may expect something equally intimate in return. The wise pastor shares her or his own story in conversation or in the pulpit only when the community will benefit from hearing it.

Emily, an Evangelical Lutheran Church in America pastor in the Minneapolis-St. Paul area, struggled to find the golden mean of boundary keeping when a member of the congregation's search committee saw herself as Emily's new best friend. According to Emily, "After I was called, she wanted to go out every week, dropped by my house on her way home, and even asked if I could babysit her children. I knew she was needy and needed to grieve her recent divorce, but I couldn't be her best friend. She couldn't understand why going to lunch with her on my day off presented a problem to me." Emily notes that when she stated her need to preserve her day off from church activities, except emergencies, her congregant responded, "Does that mean you're working when you're with me?" Although Emily didn't know quite how to respond at the time, the honest answer would have been, "Yes; that is, although our times together are fun, they are grounded in my role as pastor."

Faith says that although she enjoys good relationships with her congregants, "I never drink with them." In some settings, pastors—like the one described by Richard Lischer in an earlier chapter—will share a cocktail, glass of wine, or a beer with congregants, but wisdom dictates that one is enough in order to preserve ministerial good sense and discretion! Still, pastors need to be aware of the reality that every encounter with parishioners, even over a meal, on the golf course, or at the coffee shop, is work-related and contributes to the quality of their leadership and authority in the congregation.

Emily recalls that she didn't want to be blunt or add to her congregant's pain following her divorce, but when her congregant asked Emily to take care of her children, she gently responded, "I don't think it's appropriate for me as pastor to be your children's babysitter." Eventually, her congregant got the message and now maintains a friendly but professionally appropriate relationship with her pastor. In pondering the delicacy of expressing professional boundaries in the church, Emily, like Faith, notes their complexity:

> I have to recognize that, unlike doctors and counselors who
> see their patients or clients in a clearly defined setting, I en-

counter my parishioners in many contexts within church. The person who comes to me about a problem with her teenager or wants to be a good friend may also be on the worship committee, sing in the choir, help lead the youth group, and sit on the church board, where issues of budget and salary are decided. How I relate to people in one area shapes all the rest. So, I've learned to be careful and intentional as well as cordial and pastoral.

Bonnie sees boundaries as a spiritual issue, requiring the utmost intentionality on the part of both the pastor and her or his congregation. She notes, "When I came to this congregation, I told them that I needed two silent retreats each year and would like the budget to include monthly visits with both a counselor and a spiritual director." These have been essential, Bonnie affirms, to ensuring both the quality of her spiritual life and her congregational leadership. In her meetings with her counselor, Bonnie focuses on issues going on in the church and the quality of her responses to them. Her counselor helps her discern how she is relating to her congregation or how best to respond to a problem situation. She also consults with her counselor and spiritual director when issues at church touch her own pain and vulnerability. This helps her "get out of the way," so she can be a good pastor. Her regular meetings with her spiritual director help Bonnie maintain her prayer life so that her pastoral leadership might reflect God's vision rather than merely her own way.

Bonnie also sees healthy boundaries as a theological issue. Reflecting back on her first year in ministry, Bonnie confesses, "I thought I had to do everything; I felt so important, and they were in such need. Now I recognize that getting the job done is not all about me; God will take over when I can't. The future of the church is in God's hands and not just mine." Bonnie's approach to boundaries embodies the wisdom of the Serenity Prayer: to focus on what you can change and then let go, and let God take care of those aspects of congregational life beyond your abilities to change. Bonnie adds, "Knowing my limits and what I don't know has been helpful to boundary keeping in terms of exercising my own professional expertise. I can consult with experts, rather than responding poorly to a pastoral issue." Congregants are usually looking not for the perfect or all-knowing pastor but for a spiritual leader who will faithfully respond to their needs.

Finally, Bonnie recognizes that she must seek friendships beyond the church. "I vacation with, party with, and play with people outside the church." Like many pastors, Bonnie knows that although she cares deeply for her congregants, they are not there to respond to her personal needs. Her ability to lead is based on that delicate interplay of professional distance and personal intimacy, grounded in her sense of call.

Lyn, a United Church of Christ pastor in Lititz, Pennsylvania, also sees creative boundary keeping as a theological issue. She reminds pastors who think they are indispensable and the church can't get along without them that healthy boundaries are a matter of faith: "When you can't do something or have reached your limits, God will find somebody else to do it." This isn't a call to irresponsibility or mediocrity in ministry but the recognition that God is at work in all things, seeking abundant life even in difficult situations. Healthy pastors remember to let go and, then, let God work through laypeople and other professionals when they have reached their personal and pastoral limits. Allen, a Presbyterian pastor in suburban Baltimore, follows the same approach to boundary setting:

> I work hard and constantly seek to improve myself in ministry, but I need to remember that ultimately God is sovereign in my life and in the church. God always finds a way, even when I can't. Because God is sovereign, I need to be faithful in my calling, but I don't need to do everything. When I'm tempted to see myself as indispensible, God reminds me that [God's] in charge and I'm [God's] servant. This sets me free to serve, and also to rest.

While Lyn is grateful for the flexibility of a pastor's schedule, she has discovered two practical tools for creating healthy boundaries in ministry. First, Lyn states:

> I use my monthly report to the consistory [church board] as a way of self-monitoring. I make a list of my activities over the course of the month, noting how many sermons, visits, and meetings I have during the month. Although the consistory doesn't require a detailed report, it helps them know what I'm doing and reminds me how much I'm working and how I'm using my time. It helps me balance how many hours I work in light of my ministerial responsibilities. Sometimes it helps me notice how busy I've been and that I need to slow down.

Good boundaries require mindfulness in our availability to congregants. Ease of communication can be a blessing and a curse in ministry. After being interrupted by phone calls during supper several times, Lyn decided to invest in a second boundary keeping tool—caller ID to screen phone calls. Caller ID enables Lyn and other pastors to be more mindful in choosing when to be on duty. Other pastors keep their mealtimes and their day off sacred, except in the case of emergencies. Allen, the parent of three children under ten, states, "I treasure time with the kids and my wife. We've created a boundary around mealtimes and family nights. I don't answer the phone during mealtimes, but if a call comes in while we're eating, I take a quick look at my messages and call history after leaving the table. If it's an emergency, I excuse myself and respond to the call; if I can put it off till later that night, I go back to family night."

The son of a United Church of Christ pastor and now pastor of a suburban Philadelphia church, Jonathan describes his pastoral boundaries as being free-flowing yet relational, like jazz. Like many other professionals, including jazz musicians, Jonathan recognizes that "because my work is more than a job, most of my pleasure reading is also work reading. Much of my spare time is spent reading theology and church-related books." Jonathan continues, "My identity is interwoven with being a pastor, and as I practice ministry, there's no clear definition of space: I do my work at home, at church, and out on the community. There's no place where I'm not a pastor."

While Jonathan's boundaries are fluid and flexible, he draws the line at the Internet and social networking. He recognizes that he and other thirtysomething pastors face one great temptation in ministry: to let technology transform them into what ethicist and theologian Stanley Hauerwas has described as quivering masses of availability. He is working hard not to be accessible 24/7. Jonathan notes that in his high-tech congregation, "The e-mails fly back and forth all the time, especially from the folks who constantly use their Blackberries for communication. Initially, I responded to every message, but I've resisted getting a Blackberry or paying extra for e-mail access on my phone. This has been an important boundary for me."

Returning to the jazz analogy, Jonathan recognizes that healthy boundary keeping requires mindfulness and flexibility. "I don't draw the line. I don't separate myself into parts. I've learned to improvise, to roll with it, like jazz. Each day and week is different and calls forth different things from me. In order to stay connected and on track, like a jazz player, I rely on my partners, most particularly my wife, who regularly reminds me if she needs more of me or I look like I'm listening when I'm thinking about other things." In our conversation, Jonathan and I agreed with John Wesley's comment "The world is my parish," yet we wondered humorously "what Wesley's wife thought about it." And we agreed that even a fully integrated ministry requires moments of rest, recuperation, and disengagement.

Ray, a United Church of Christ pastor of two rural congregations, confesses, "I'm not so good at setting time and space boundaries. I always think of things that need to be done. And, because I do most of my work at home, it's hard to separate work time from home time. Holding regular office hours at the church hasn't worked because people rarely stop by the churches I pastor." Ray finds joy in working at home, however. "I can take a break during sermon preparation and do laundry or listen to the news on NPR or CNN, or if my mind's worn out, I play my dulcimer, Celtic harp, or recorder." Nevertheless, Ray keeps a weekly log of the hours he works to monitor his workload. "I categorize my hours according to different tasks—worship, preaching, pastoral calls, newsletter. I work thirty-five to seventy hours each week but try to work less after a busy week." Ray tries to combine hospital visits, sometimes two hours away from his rural congregations, with shopping or an outing with his wife, commenting, "That way I feel a sense of joy, combining the challenging task of visitation with a pleasurable time with my wife."

Creative Wisdom on Boundaries in Ministry

Several important theological and practical insights emerge from the comments of these and scores of other new pastors with whom I have spoken. These insights serve as best practices for pastors seeking healthy boundaries.

First, recognize that boundaries reflect your calling and theology of ministry. Because pastors are called to equip the church, everything we do should be seen as supporting the well-being of our congregants and contributing to God's shalom in our world. Our beliefs set our boundaries. Called by God, we are accountable to God for the use of our gifts in ministry. This accountability means more than "First, do no harm," although this is an important maxim for physicians and pastors alike. It is also about doing "something beautiful for God" (Mother Teresa) in ministry.

Second, healthy boundaries involve the interplay of self-care and care for others. Healthy boundary keeping involves self-monitoring and intentionality in relationship to our congregants, grounded in questions such as:

+ How do I feel about this congregant—positively or negatively?
+ Am I am appropriately intimate, yet differentiated, in my actions and language?
+ How am I feeling physically, spiritually, relationally, and emotionally, and how is my well-being shaping the quality of my ministry?
+ Am I involved in complicated relationships—such as having a congregant's daughter babysit or a congregant do home improvements—that may harm my ministry in the long run?
+ Do I place God and my congregants first in my pastoral relationships?

Third, healthy boundaries require an awareness of how we use our time in ministry. While we cannot fully manage that time, we can be intentional and choose to go on a retreat, take an extra day off, or spend more time with family following a stressful period in ministry or after Christmas and Easter. Creative boundaries involve monitoring our hours as well as our tasks. While some tasks are essential, others may be optional. Consider the following questions regarding your use of time in ministry.

+ Am I efficient in my office work?
+ Do I spend time on projects that I should delegate to others?
+ How is my time divided between ministry, study, family life, friendships, self-care, and spiritual practices? Is it balanced or unbalanced?
+ How many hours have I worked in each of the last four weeks? Is this too much or too little time for my responsibilities at church and home?

Fourth, healthy boundaries call us to live prayerfully, constantly praying for our congregation, specific congregants, and challenging situations. When we relate to our congregants prayerfully, our own needs fall into the background.

Fifth, and this is also a matter of prayerful self-awareness, healthy pastors get their emotional and relational needs met outside the church. Do you have projects, hobbies, and friendships that take you beyond congregational life? If not, where might you explore new relationships and hobbies?

Listening to Your Life

Healthy boundaries involve the dynamic interplay of the pastor's inward and outward journeys. We are called to *listen to our lives* (Frederick Buechner) and then *let our lives speak* (Parker Palmer) in ways that embody God's wisdom and love in our professional lives.

Listening to our lives, as psychiatrist Gerald May notes, involves *pausing, noticing, opening, yielding and stretching,* before we *respond* in creative acts of ministerial leadership and pastoral care. This practice may take fifteen minutes or more, depending on your life situation.

First, take a few gentle centering breaths, noticing and letting go of any discomfort and stress, physical or emotional.

Second, after a few minutes of prayerful relaxation, begin to look at your ministry, reflecting on the following:

+ How are my current congregational relationships? Are any problematic? Am I too close to, or too distant from, certain members?
+ How is my spiritual life? Do I take time for prayer and meditation?
+ How am I balancing the many commitments of ministry? What am I focusing on? What am I neglecting?

You may choose to write these responses in a journal, noting God's movements in your responses to these questions.

Third, take a few moments to open to God's creative wisdom. Ask for guidance in responding to any issues that emerge.

Fourth, in the quiet, listen for any wisdom or guidance that emerges about steps you might take to respond more healthfully or creatively to relationships and boundaries.

Fifth, prayerfully make a commitment to initiate new pastoral behaviors or to change behaviors or attitudes in ministry.

Conclude with a prayer of thanksgiving for God's guidance in your life and your calling to be a pastoral leader.

CHAPTER 6

THE
INNOVATIVE
PASTOR

Do not be conformed to this world, but be transformed by
the renewing of your minds, so that you may discern what is
the will of God—what is good and acceptable and perfect.
—ROMANS 12:2

WHEN A PASTOR IS CALLED TO A NEW CONGREGATION,
everything changes for the congregation and pastor alike. This
is especially true in the ministries of newly ordained pastors
who are making the transition from seminary studies to congregational leadership. As I have noted before, this is a season
of firsts for the novice pastor, but it is also a season of change
and transformation for the congregation that he or she will
serve. Common wisdom holds that pastors, whether experienced in ministry or beginning their first call, should make few
changes during their first year of ministry; after all, their arrival
causes enough "disturbance in the force," to use the language of
the *Star Wars* movies. Their vocation during this time is to get
to know the congregants and to gain their trust and respect
before making any significant changes in the life of the church.

Generally speaking, this is good advice. There is an intimate relationship between trust and transformation: congregants accept the guidance of their pastor and his or her visions of change better once they trust the pastor's expertise and care for themselves and the well-being of the congregation to which they belong. As one pastor said, "After I'd accompanied a few congregants in their final days and ministered to their families in times of grief and crisis, then I felt comfortable sharing my vision of where the church should go." Still, many congregations are ready for change when a new pastor arrives. They want leadership, and they hope that a new pastor, even one just recently ordained, can breathe new life into the dry bones of their congregation's life. As one North Carolina United Church of Christ pastor reports, "The chair of the board's first counsel to me was, 'Be a leader.'" Without a vision for the future and someone to bring new and creative energy to congregational life, congregations lose vitality and mission and soon begin to decline both spiritually and numerically.

Transformation is at the heart of the biblical story. Paul counsels the church in Rome to be transformed, that is, to embody a new vision and way of life in contrast to their past beliefs and behaviors. The Hebraic understanding of God portrays the Holy One moving through history, constantly challenging the people to greater fidelity and enlarged visions for the nation and the world. God proclaims, "Behold, I do a new thing," and challenges the people to mirror God's own adventures in social and spiritual transformation. Although deeply rooted in the wisdom of the Hebraic tradition, Jesus saw his vocation as inviting his people—and those beyond the Jewish tradition—to new pathways of discipleship. Jesus's words, "You have heard that it was said . . . but I say to you," were a call to spiritual transformation that embraces both belief and action (Matt. 5:21–48).

Even the most traditional rural congregations recognize that they live in novel times in which their willingness to embrace

God's transforming vision is essential to their growth and revitalization. In this time of radical change in society and congregational life, even the most deliberate pastors are called to become change agents who gently and intentionally urge their congregations to embrace new ways of being faithful to Jesus. In this chapter, I will share the stories of three pastors who began to make significant changes in their respective congregations in the early stages of their first ministerial call. While many pastors will move more carefully in the area of congregational transformation, their stories remind us that change is inevitable in congregational life and that the simple act of beginning a new ministry alters the dynamics of a congregation. These new pastors model an approach that balances innovation and challenge with affirmation of congregational traditions. They recognize that resistance is inevitable and that those who resist a pastor's vision are often inspired by their love of congregational traditions or their own alternative visions of the congregation's future. These innovative pastors seek reconciliation with those who resist their vision as part of their commitment to nurturing the mission of the whole body of Christ.

Leadership by Wandering Around

Paul Eyer is known on the streets as "the walking pastor." A second-career pastor who spent a number of years practicing law and working in politics prior to seminary, he is known by his daily walks throughout his downtown Lancaster, Pennsylvania, neighborhood. Baptist by upbringing, Paul experienced the call to ministry in midlife. Following graduation from Lancaster Theological Seminary, Paul was called to be pastor of a small, urban congregation at the edge of downtown Lancaster. Once a thriving neighborhood congregation, St. Luke's United Church of Christ had largely lost touch with its changing, multiethnic environment. Most of its members commuted to church on Sundays but did little to reach out to the growing number of Hispanic and refugee families in the immediate neighborhood. They believed that their programs and worship had little to offer the changing neighborhood—that is, until they called the walking pastor to be their spiritual leader.

Paul and Jackie, another newly ordained United Church of Christ pastor, settled in a row house just a few blocks from St. Luke's shortly after their marriage. When he was called to be the pastor of St. Luke's, Paul made it clear that he would be a pastor to the neighborhood as well as the congregation. From the very beginning of his ministry, Paul walked the neighborhood, sometimes solo, but often with his husky, Jake, doing what he describes as "foot-powered evangelism." Indeed, evangelism is at the heart of Paul's understanding of ministry. Theologically progressive, Paul is also committed to sharing the good news of Jesus wherever he goes. Paul has found that Jake is a "church magnet." Adults and kids in the neighborhood come off their porches, pet the dog, and engage in conversation, and Paul introduces himself as the pastor of the neighborhood church. Typically, Paul begins his conversations with the words, "I'm Paul Eyer. I live and work in the neighborhood, and I'm pastor of St. Luke's Church on Marietta Avenue." Paul reports that, from these casual and occasionally wide-ranging conversations, a number of people have found their way to St. Luke's. Paul notes, "It helps to identify myself as a neighbor."

When Paul arrived at St. Luke's, the congregation had very limited contact with the neighborhood. Paul knew that he had to raise the congregation's profile in the neighborhood while inviting members to become his partners in mission to the community, if the congregation were to grow in outreach, vitality, and participation. From the very beginning, Paul made it clear to his congregation that "evangelism would be a priority" in his ministry. Evangelism requires a sustained effort, and Paul is constantly on the move, walking through the neighborhood, participating in neighborhood civic groups, and opening the church doors to newcomers through programs and hospitality.

Jesus taught that from a mustard seed, a great plant will grow. This principle is also true for congregational transformation: from small beginnings, new life emerges, and as an isolated congregation begins to reach out tentatively to its neighborhood, members discover unexpected signs of hope. Changes that seem ordinary and modest from an outsider's viewpoint may feel like a leap of faith to a congregation set in its ways. Paul's first programmatic outreach was quite modest from his perspective and involved providing candy for the neighborhood kids on Halloween. Dressed in their liturgical robes, Paul and his wife Jackie passed out candy to the children walking by the church that evening. They opened the church doors and turned on the lights of the sanctuary, just a few feet from the sidewalk, and let people of all ages enter the sanctuary, most for the first time. At first, many of the parents asked if his clerical robe was a Halloween costume. A few more asked, "Are you a priest?" When Paul responded that he was St. Luke's pastor, a number of them requested prayers for friends or family members. In the ensuing weeks, several of the families stopped in for worship at St. Luke's.

A few weeks later, the congregation offered a family-friendly movie night to the neighborhood. Much to the surprise of members who believed that no one in the neighborhood would come to their church, over seventy-five people filled the church's social hall. The response within the congregation was equally startling, Paul recalls. For some members, the movie night opened their eyes to the community and challenged their belief that none of the neighbors would ever come to church. Paul quite humbly admits that these are small steps, but small steps can be a big deal for a congregation that had given up on reaching its neighborhood.

Paul's endeavors have, of course, been met with resistance by some church members. While congregants often say they want to respond to the needs of their neighborhood, the concrete realities of growing building usage and changed demographics often lead to conflict. Conflict over a changing mission is nothing new in Christian history, however. The early church struggled theologically and ethically with its calling to go out into the Gentile world. Like many of today's urban churches, the early Christians asked, "How can we accept their cultural and ethnic values and remain true to our tradition? How much change can we embrace without losing our core identity? How can we reach out to the community and still keep the building tidy?" As one old-time member lamented when new people of diverse ethnic groups began to attend the congregation, "We're no longer St. Luke's." Such concerns about the changing face of a congregation and building usage and care (in the case of St. Luke's, the issue was the kitchen) are legitimate but must be informed by the church's mandate to reach out to the world, whether in the neighborhood or across the globe.

Healthy leadership calls a congregation to become a new creation, building on its past and leaning toward God's vision for the future. Paul notes that reading William Chris Hobgood's *Welcoming Resistance*, a textbook assigned for one my classes, helped prepare him for the conflicts that emerged as he sought to expand the congregation's mission.[1] Community involvement leads to resistance, because community outreach challenges congregations to transformation, and all transformation involves both gain and loss for a community. As he looks at his tenure at St. Luke's, the ever-optimistic Paul counsels new pastors to "anticipate and welcome resistance whenever they make even the smallest changes in congregational life. Don't be afraid of resistance." Paul also counsels new pastors to "make sure that congregational leaders are aware of what you're doing and get involved in your projects." Involvement by church leaders ensures that outreach is a community endeavor rather than merely the pastor's pet project.

Spirit-Centered Unity

Elaine Moyer was in many ways the perfect fit for her current Evangelical Lutheran Church in America–United Church of Christ congregation in the farm community of Ickesburg, Pennsylvania. A midlife pastor, she had grown up on the family poultry farm, which she helped manage prior to attending seminary. Elaine is a self-described conservative, both theologically and politically, whose media outlet of choice is Fox News. The simple maxim "To preach the gospel and love the people" describes how she understands her call to ministry. An innovator, she asks the people to take little steps in worship and practice that often lead to great advances in faithful mission.

Shortly after Elaine arrived, a church patriarch pulled her aside and told her, "We need leadership." Elaine has been the right leader for the right time, and her leadership is grounded in love for her people. In describing her work, Elaine is effusive: "It's a joy to be here. God has amazing ways of bringing you here! This is a great opportunity to be pastor to a good bunch of people."

Elaine had been called to pastor two congregations that had shared pastoral leadership for nearly fifty years. Yet, from the beginning, Elaine recognized that these faithful rural congregations, one in many ways, needed to find a sense of common purpose and unity in Christ. Their buildings less than a block away from one another, the ELCA and UCC congregants met together for social events, shared worship for two months each summer and winter. Every four months, they traded worship times, alternating between 9:00 a.m. and 11:00 a.m. Although they functioned as one congregation in a variety of ways, they resisted meeting together every Sunday. As Elaine notes, "They hated to see a church closed." Further, the UCC service was fairly informal, while the ELCA service reflected a high liturgy.

Over the years, the United Church of Christ congregation had dwindled to an average worship attendance of fewer than twenty people. With a shrinking budget, building upkeep had become a challenge. One Sunday, as Elaine recalls, an eighty-eight-year-old elder at the UCC church whispered in her ear, "We need to talk. It's time to bring us together."

Still, bringing together two congregations, most of whose members knew each other well and who shared virtually everything from worship leadership to pastoral care, was no easy matter. With the support of both congregations' leadership, Elaine convened a committee made up of people from each church. She also sought the support of judicatory officials from the Evangelical Lutheran Church in America and the United Church of Christ. Elaine knew that obstacles lay ahead in the process: each congregation would have to give up something in order to claim greater unity in Christ. The ELCA congregation would have to become open to more informal worship. The United Church of Christ congregation would have to let go of its beloved building.

A person of great prayer for whom Jesus is truly a personal companion, Elaine had a deep intuition while she was reading her Bible one day. "I had a vision of what [the united churches] would look like. We would be like an umbrella with both groups sharing the same stem as we journeyed into one building." Elaine realized that the unity of two congregations was first a pastoral issue and, then, an issue of administration and logistics. Therefore, she "did a lot of talking with the people," listening and reassuring them, and sharing her vision that together they could be more faithful to God's mission in their community. After several months of meeting and sharing, the two congregations chose by nearly unanimous affirmation to become one body of Christ in Ickesburg.

When considering uniting the two congregations in one worship service, a major concern was joining the two choirs. But, as usual, Elaine sought a win-win approach. The two long-standing choir directors now rotate leadership from month to month. The churches have also adopted new hymnals to celebrate a new day in their lives.

Coming together in mutual ministry has enabled the new congregation to refurbish the building, making it accessible to people with handicaps. Whereas some church unions lead to diminished total attendance, the new congregation is larger, more dynamic, and more committed to the community.

Elaine shared several words of counsel for new pastors who seek to be congregational change agents. She recalls the words of Ava Blackwell, former director of admissions at Lancaster Theological Seminary: "Go visit your people in their homes." While this might be challenging in the culture of urban congregations, this advice created a bond between Elaine and her congregants. Elaine placed a clipboard in each church, noting that she was free every afternoon for conversation. The response was overwhelming, and people eagerly signed up for her to visit. In this same spirit, Elaine counsels, "The pastor needs to know her people. You have to have a relationship of mutual trust." Pastors consistently note that once they gain their congregation's trust as a leader who is seeking the congregation's highest good, congregants become more open to pastoral initiatives, even though they may involve significant congregational changes.

Elaine suggests that small town pastors "go to where the people are—sporting events, school plays, local events." Like Father Tim in Jan Karon's Mitford novels, Elaine has become a fixture at the local coffee shop, often dropping in for breakfast, a cup of coffee, or just to say hello.[2] At the heart of Elaine's counsel is something essential to faithful and effective ministry: "Know your people. You've got to live with them. Regardless of your vision, you need to know how they feel. I needed to listen and experience what giving up their church meant to them." Elaine knew that even though uniting the two congregations created new opportunities for vital worship and mission in the community, she still had to honor the experiences of her congregants. In *The Four Seasons of Ministry*, Katherine Epperly and I quote Gordon Forbes, pastor emeritus of Westmoreland United Church of Christ in Bethesda, Maryland, who says we are called to "first be a pastor," even when we are called to be a change agent.[3]

Living by a Vision

Biblical theologian and scholar Marcus Borg describes Jesus as a spirit person whose lived experience of God enabled him to reveal God's presence to others. I believe that today's pastors are also called to be spirit people whose sense of God's presence through practices such as prayer, meditation, and prophetic hospitality invites congregants to deepen their own spiritual lives and commitment to God's vision of shalom. Monica Dawkins-Smith fits the vocation of pastor as spirit person: she was called to ministry through a mystical experience,[4] she anchors her life in an intimate relationship with Jesus, and she experiences her call as a new pastor as the ongoing quest to discover God's vision for her life.

Monica recalls her first experience at the historic Salem United Church of Christ (Old Salem Church) in Harrisburg, Pennsylvania. Jamaican in ancestry, she was called to fill in one Sunday at what was then an aging German Reformed congregation. As she preached, she had a vision that literally took her breath away. She saw what the church was called to be in its changing neighborhood. "I saw the church as God intended it to be, filled with people of all ethnicities and ages, African Americans, Latinos and Latinas, refugees, men, women, and children, [people] of all sexual orientations." A year later, she was called to pastor Old Salem Church, and under her direction, this historic church is embracing God's new creation.

Monica did not initially jump at the call to serve Salem UCC. Instead of choosing to be installed as its permanent pastor, she chose to be supply pastor for a year in order for the congregation and her to discern whether her leadership was part of God's call for them. Monica had a dream for the congregation, and she wanted her dream of a multicultural congregation to be in sync with the congregation's aspirations. Monica saw a new congregation emerging from Old Salem, not to supplant the historic congregation but to reach out to a diverse community that surrounded the congregation. Monica remembers that the vote to call her as pastor and teacher was rather close because people feared she would neglect the existing congregation as she worked to form a new one. These fears have been unfounded: as the new church begins its afternoon service, the existing congregation's morning service is growing in vitality and participation.

When she, an innovative entrepreneur and an African American woman, accepted the call to a stable, primarily white congregation, Monica knew that she was taking a risk. But adventurous living has been at heart of her vocational journey, and she testifies, "I followed the call, not knowing where it would lead."

Monica, like Paul and Elaine, sees spiritual leadership as a matter of faithful innovation rather than organizational maintenance. While leading a revitalization process in an aging and numerically declining congregation, she was also initiating a new congregational start in the same building, aimed at downtown Harrisburg's diverse cultural, ethnic, and lifestyle communities. In the process, the existing congregation has experienced a transformation of heart: where once they were reluctant to support the new congregation, now they embrace God's new vision in their midst. This new congregation, Journeys, welcomes with open arms seekers, people who have been wounded by the church, and those who feel formal and liturgical worship is irrelevant to their spiritual quest. Monica has learned to be an agile preacher and worship leader. In the morning, she preaches a fairly traditional—that is, if anything Monica does is traditional—sermon to her German Reformed UCC congregation. In the afternoon, she "breaks it down," as she says, through interactive sermons with the more informal congregation.

Like Paul and Elaine, Monica recognizes that growing a congregation is a matter of relationship. As she birthed the vision of Journeys, Monica was omnipresent in downtown Harrisburg, going to art shows, coffee shops, political and social events, and service clubs. As she witnesses, "I kept on inviting and then inviting again," first to informal Bible studies and now to the Sunday afternoon service. The vision of Journeys, now being realized each Sunday and throughout the week, was to "Rediscover God, Find Hope, Find Acceptance—At Last."

Still, Monica did not abandon the existing congregation. The same spirit of hospitality and initiative that characterized her work with Journeys is evident in her pastoral care of Old Salem UCC. She accepted the people where they were; got to know their hopes, dreams, and fears; and then called them to new possibilities. Indeed, Old Salem's spiritual adventures were grounded in a new approach to prayer. With its building located on a major thoroughfare, literally only a few feet from the street, the congregation chose to erect a prayer box that invited the prayer requests of passersby. As Monica recalls, she and the congregation recognized that "not everyone may want to come to church, but everyone wants prayer." She listened to her congregants' visions, invited a church member to build the prayer box, and dedicated it in worship, laying hands on the box and inviting the generally quiet congregation to offer intercessory prayers. Initially, members wondered if anyone would notice the prayer box or even contribute a prayer request. To their surprise and now weekly anticipation, the requests came in handfuls and still keep coming, and have become central to the congregation's intercessory prayer time each Sunday.

The prayer box morphed into a prayer garden adjacent to the sidewalk. A bench was erected, providing a spot for people to pray, meditate, or rest awhile in the midst of a busy day or on their way to and from the hospital down the street. Creating a prayerful space in the midst of downtown has transformed this once inward-looking congregation. It has, as Monica asserts, "taken them one step further from where they were and has brought the congregation together around a spiritual task." Monica affirms that transformation begins with small steps:

"You don't need to start big, but a sense of unity is foundational for moving ahead. Growth happens when a pastor is able to lead from a place of unity and a vision of outreach that the congregation can rally around."

Monica's counsel to transformational pastors is, first, "Do your inner work, keep nurturing your call, and find what sustains you for the challenges of spiritual leadership and congregational change." Ministry needs to be revitalized and sustained over the long haul by a commitment to prayer, devotional reading, and meditation. Second, she advises new pastors that leadership comes from joining acceptance and listening with a process of reframing. After listening and recognizing where a congregation has been and what stands in the way of growth, "Help them reframe things. Invite them to go further one step at a time. Look for places where the congregation can join as one, and move ahead from there." This is wise counsel for new pastors. Our personal and congregational calls never come to people and congregations in the abstract; they come to concrete, flesh and blood, limited, and sometimes fearful communities—like Corinth, Ephesus, Philippi, and Salem UCC. God calls us where we are, casting a vision of what we can become if we are attentive to God's emerging guidance. Much to their surprise, many congregations discover that what they thought were limitations are really the womb of new possibilities. A wise new pastor listens well to the people and to God's inspiration moving through the community of faith; challenges and invites without judging; and faithfully accompanies a congregation each step of the way, providing encouragement and reassurance.

The Creative Wisdom of Innovation

Creative congregational transformation involves the dynamic and intimate interplay of order and novelty, tradition and innovation. To imagine future possibilities, first you need to know where you are. Possibility thinking, as abstract as it may seem, must be grounded in the concreteness of congregational life. Jesus recognized that five loaves and two fish, all the resources the disciples had at the moment, could not feed a multitude. But Jesus also saw possibility where others saw a dead end. Five loaves and two fish, like the mustard seed of Jesus's parable, can become the foundation for life-nourishing mission.

Imagining a congregation's future has a number of components that may emerge over several weeks or months in a pastor's first congregational call. The point is not to hurry innovation, but to let it emerge relationally and organically in the interaction of God's vision, a pastor's initiative, and a congregation's unique gifts.

First, take time to get to know your congregation. Listen to congregants' stories, ask them about their practices of faith, explore what gives them joy in congregational life, and invite them to dream about their congregation's future. This gentle spiritual ethnography, inspired by the process of appreciative inquiry, identifies congregational values, energy, and joy. I view this conversational process as an act of imagination, because the pastor needs both to hear the words, people's hopes and concerns, and to look deeply into the congregants' experiences, identifying God-moments that may have eluded them. While this process can be done in a group setting and no doubt should eventually be the foundation for congregational visioning and strategic planning, one-to-one conversations build trust, intimacy, and partnership between a pastor and her or his congregants.

Second, take time to meditate on what you have heard, exploring both the dreams and the impediments to their realization. Recognize your congregation's apparent limitations in imagination, finances, energy, location, and demographics. To midwife possibilities for faithfulness and innovation in the congregation, the pastor must be grounded in, though not limited by, the concrete realities of congregational life.

Third, let your imagination roam as you ask God to provide you with a creative vision for your congregation. What images, scriptures, pictures, and words emerge from your openness to God? You may choose in this process to explore multiple media and multiple intelligences through journaling, drawing, singing, writing poetry, or physical activity. Then, as a prelude to sharing your vision with congregational leaders, take time to prayerfully open yourself to God's guidance in relating your vision to your particular setting. Ask for God's creative wisdom for sharing the vision with potential partners who can shape the vision with you. Remember that visions are always fluid and in process, and that congregational visioning and embodied action may go in a different direction from what either pastor or congregation initially imagined.

CHAPTER 7

DEATH NEVER TAKES A HOLIDAY FOR PASTORS AND CONGREGATIONS

For everything there is a season, and a time for every matter under heaven: a time to be born, and a time to die.

—Ecclesiastes 3:1–2

Sharon, a newly ordained Presbyterian pastor of a suburban Ohio congregation, confessed, "I never realized that I'd be doing so many funerals during my first year of ministry. I took a death and dying class in seminary, but when I had my first death, I felt like I was starting from scratch. I was worried I would make a big mistake in meeting with a family I'd only met a few times and in doing the service. Thank God, the local funeral director showed me where to stand at the graveside, or I might have fallen in!"

Jennifer, a United Church of Christ pastor in a town-and-country congregation in Maryland, almost did fall into a recently dug grave. She vividly remembers going to the graveside, misjudging the placement of the artificial grass, after which she tripped and nearly fell into the grave! She recalls joking afterward with some of her congregants, "I had to make sure it was six feet deep." More experienced and wiser, Jennifer now routinely "feels around the head of the casket in order to know where I can step!" A suburban Chicago United Methodist pastor, Matt admits that while he is adept at responding to deaths pastorally and ritually within his community, he needs to "learn to care for himself when he has to respond to the needs of the bereaved. I do it well, but I feel a lot of stress." These comments were echoed in a new pastors' seminar focusing on Lenten spirituality. All the participants nodded in agreement when one member admitted that she was unsure "how I could fit in one or more funeral services along with everything else I have to do during Lent."

Death never takes a holiday, even in the busiest seasons of the Christian year, nor does it wait for us to be fully prepared as professionals. The mortality rate will remain at 100 percent regardless of our medical interventions or holistic health practices. As my field education mentor, Disciples of Christ pastor George Tolman, said in a sermon some thirty years ago, "Life is risky business; no one gets out alive." In some congregations, pastors will be overwhelmed by the deaths of a whole generation of beloved members in the space of a year or two. Other new pastors will go for more than a year before their first funeral, unconsciously assuming that there is something exceptional about their congregation, and then face five funerals in the course of a month. Yet, how we as pastors respond to crises in our congregation can deepen our faith, our relationships with our congregants, and the faith of the congregation as a whole. Truly, as Martin Luther asserted, "In the midst of life, we are surrounded by death." But faithful excellence in ministry is also grounded in Luther's complementary affirmation, "In the midst of death, we are surrounded by life." Perhaps nowhere is our theology and professional practice more closely connected than when we face the realities of death and our responsibilities as spiritual leaders, shepherds, and healers.

While no one theology of death and dying undergirds faithful excellence in ministry, effective pastors cultivate a theological vision that inspires and sustains their pastoral responses to death and bereavement. At the very least, pastors are challenged to integrate head, heart, and hands in responding to suffering and mortality. While theological reflection is not always appropriate in the wake of a sudden death, in the course of an extended death, or after the rawness of grief has subsided, pastors are summoned to be both theologians and healers of their congregations as they face questions from children and adults alike. Virtually every pastor has heard questions such as these:

+ Where is my little brother now?
+ Why did God take my sister (daughter, mother, father) away from me?
+ What did I do to deserve this?
+ Why us? We lived a good life and were faithful.
+ Could it be that God is punishing me for my divorce?
+ Is my father in heaven or hell, since he wasn't a Christian?
+ Did God have a purpose behind all this pain?
+ How will my family get along without me?

While we may not presume to have clear answers to such questions, most new pastors avoid answers that blame the victim or cut off discussion by giving theological answers prematurely or by silencing any doubt, either in our congregants or in ourselves.

Drawing on tradition, our theology of death finds inspiration in the interplay of cross and resurrection in Christian life. The cross of Jesus reminds us of the universality of suffering and the sense of abandonment that often accompanies death. Yet, the vulnerability and sense of abandonment found in Jesus's invocation of Psalm 22, "My God, my God, why have you forsaken me?" is met with the affirmation of Psalm 23: "Even though I walk through the darkest valley, I fear no evil; for you are with me; your rod and your staff—they comfort me."

Death is universal and can't be denied. Yet the reality of death is abstract and purely academic for many new pastors until they face their first death, either in a CPE (clinical pastoral education) setting, in the congregation, or in their own family. It is then, as one pastor admits, that you discover, "You can't go around the valley; you must go through it, in order to experience resurrection."

To claim resurrection hope too soon is to be tempted to see Jesus's death and our own mortality as an illusion or merely an inconvenience on the road to resurrection. Celebrating too soon denies the uncertainty and everyday suffering present within our congregations. It gives in to our temptations to fix either what cannot be fixed or what must be borne with patience and faith in the unseen. Every Holy Week, I try to take a Holy Saturday retreat in order to claim the uncertainty of resurrection and embrace my own feelings of doubt and anxiety when I face my own aging, mortality, and serious illness within my family. In the midst of life, there is no assurance of a happy ending, but there is the wondrous promise of resurrection, of new and transformed life bursting forth despite the witness of the medical chart and funeral preparations.

In moments when death and life intersect, new pastors have the opportunity, despite their own feelings of fear and trembling, to enter the lives of their congregants when they are most vulnerable. In so doing, they become Christ's ambassadors of realistic, hard-won hope and authentic, life-changing companionship. As witnesses to the promise of new life in the midst of death, new pastors can proclaim, "Christ is risen. . . . Nothing can separate us from the love of God," even though the pain of Good Friday remains.

Encounters with Death

Now in her second year as pastor of a small United Church of Christ congregation in Eastern Pennsylvania, Wanda asserts that as a new pastor, "You have to roll with what comes. You can't always anticipate things. In fact, during my first three months, I had seven deaths and funerals. It was almost like they were waiting for the shepherd to come." She recalls, "There were a few deaths in the months before I came, and the survivors were still grieving. In this congregation where everyone is related, everyone was touched by these deaths." When I asked Wanda how she survived so much death in her first weeks of ministry, she responded that "she regularly met with three other female colleagues, two of whom were also new to ministry, and our support for one another helped me get through."

Paul's first encounter with death as a congregational minister is a poignant reminder that death never takes a holiday. The pastor of a downtown United Church of Christ congregation in Lancaster, Pennsylvania, Paul recounts, "When I first began at St. Luke's, I ministered with a young man, the son of one of the congregation's more prominent families, who was slowly and painfully dying of cancer." In the months preceding his death, Paul had regularly visited the young man as well as his parents. When the death finally came on Christmas morning, Paul was presented with a dilemma: "Should I drop everything and visit the family, or should I stay with my own family?" Paul explains, "I might have done it differently today, but I stayed home with my family. I had done a lot of pastoral work with the family prior to the death, and I felt that they would be OK and would understand my decision." As it was, when the family scheduled the funeral for later in Christmas week, Paul chose to cancel some of his holiday plans.

As he ponders his vocation as pastor in moments of death and bereavement, Paul asserts:

My primary role is first to provide comfort by my presence and then give a sense of hope as God's gift to us, communicated in a meaningful and personal way, to the bereaved. Theology sustains us in times of death and grief. Whether in ... conversation with one who is dying or with her or his family, I express resurrection hope. While I don't fully know what we can expect in the afterlife, I believe that the loved one is reunited with God. Salvation is in God's hands, and I believe that God seeks to draw all people to himself.

Kate, a Presbyterian pastor in Michigan, recognized the interplay of theology and pastoral care when she ministered to a long-time member of the church whose forty-year-old daughter had committed suicide. Kate recalls:

When she asked me, "Where is Susan now?" I knew the question wasn't academic. She wanted to know whether suicide would exclude Susan from God's love—whether her beloved daughter was in heaven or hell. I didn't have an articulate theological response, and that was a good thing. I told her that I believed that God is love and God's love surrounds Susan. That was enough for her in the face of the comments of some of her more conservative relatives.

In such moments, the pastor is not only a pastoral care giver and priest to the faith community. She is also its theological shepherd whose words give hope and comfort for the grief that lies ahead. More than once I have heard my congregants assert, in contrast to more dualistic heaven-and-hell scenarios invoked by their Christian relatives, "My pastor says that Jim is in God's hands, and that's good enough for me." In such wilderness moments, pastors become the living voice of God, sharing, sometimes with fear and trembling, their vision of God in ways that bring healing rather than despair. Pastoral presence is essential when death is near, but a healing word, a positive theological affirmation, can give hope after the funeral is over and for the challenges ahead.

Kent, a theologically conservative United Methodist pastor, recognizes that his first task is to be pastoral. He affirms, "I can't claim to say whether the deceased is in heaven or hell, so I share my belief that God loves and seeks to save everyone, and we must leave the future of unbelieving relatives in God's hands."

Jackie, Paul's spouse and herself a United Church of Christ pastor, recalls experiencing an intuition that led her to visit a congregant who had been physically declining. "I had a sense that I should visit. Although I had other calls to make, I didn't want him to die alone. I went in, said a few prayers, and had a sense of awareness that the end was near. And, then, he died." In the weeks prior to his death, Jackie had visited him a few times and had gotten to know him. She remembers him saying to her when he was first asked if he wanted a pastoral visit, "If you're willing to listen, I'm willing to talk." Jackie notes, "It's tough to get the phone call announcing that one of your congregants is dying. You have to drop everything. But in such moments, people are closer to the heart and speak from it." Jackie is grateful that her experiences in CPE enabled her to "respond as a professional to dying people and their families and to be a nonanxious presence who can help simply by being there and listening." In her words, "My year in CPE gave me tools to deal with my fear of not being able to fix things for people in adversity as well theological, psychological, and relational issues I would encounter in the parish." Jackie also recalled that CPE taught her ways to care for herself while she was caring for others. Jackie remembers, "In CPE, I would go to the neonatal unit and just rock babies after a hard day. In CPE, I learned that I had to take care of myself in order to care for others." She still looks for healthy ways of caring for herself to replenish the emotional resources she needs to care for others. "Finding a larger perspective on life-and-death issues, as well as changes

I need to make in my week when a death occurs, enables me to look beyond my stress and trust that God is with me."

Jennifer affirms Jackie's recognition of the importance of CPE for her own work related to death and dying. "I'd have been unequipped without it," she says.

Betsy, a Mennonite pastor in Denver, recognizes the importance of theology in responding to death but asserts that words alone cannot minister to the dying and grieving. She notes, "Congregants appreciate the fact that you're with them when they need it. It isn't so much what you say, but that you're present. I realize that at such moments, they just need help and companionship, and I'm there for them," whether at the bedside, while surgery is taking place, or after a death. In such moments, even if we give little explicit theological consolation, our nonanxious presence represents God's deep and abiding care and the hope that all will be well, despite these present shadows of grief and fear.

The Grieving Pastor

Death doesn't take into consideration what is going on in a pastor's personal life. Often, we must deal with our own grief as we deal with the grief of our congregants. Robin, a United Church of Christ pastor in Northwest Ohio, tells of having to perform a funeral immediately after her own mother's death. Robin describes the planning and the service as "a healing experience." She notes that while her mother's funeral reflected the wishes of her stepfather, the priest's homily said nothing about who her mother was as a person. In Robin's words, "When I got back, I had a funeral I had to do. I had not met the woman before; although she was a saint of the church, she had spent the last few years living with her son in another state. In talking with her son, I learned that she was a lot like my own mother. I listened to her son. As I put together my sermon, I prayerfully tried to capture who she was. I was reminded of my mother and the life she led." Robin can identify with the apostle Paul's affirmation, "My grace is sufficient for you, for power is made perfect in weakness . . . for whenever I am weak, then I am strong" (2 Cor. 12:9–10). She concludes, "I could relate to their grief because I was experiencing my own." Like the wounded healer, an image popularized by Henri Nouwen, Robin discovered that her wounds could be openings for God's grace to flow through her in healing ways.

The grieving pastor often learns that she must accept her congregants' personal support while maintaining appropriate professional boundaries. Congregants want to reach out, and accepting their care for us as pastors in times of grief and illness is appropriate. Robin says, "Being a pastor has allowed me to learn to let my community care for me, while keeping my ministerial boundaries. They gently held me, as I grieved my own mother's death, with cards and hugs and kind words. It was a quiet and comforting care, grounded in our mutual experiences of grief throughout our lives." Robin continues her reflections on grief and ministry: "I knew I was still a pastor, yet I could allow myself to be cared for, to hold in tension my vocation as pastor with their desire to reach out, because they knew my family was far away in New England."

Pastors must learn not only to give but also to appropriately receive in the dynamic call and response of ministry. If we only give and never receive, we turn our backs on the graceful care of others. Professional boundaries are essential, but they are not intended to imprison the pastor or stifle the healthy love of congregants. Even Jesus accepted the care of Mary and Martha and grieved greatly at their brother Lazarus's death.

Pat, a United Church of Christ pastor, recognizes that ministry with the dying can be healing for both pastor and congregants. Recently, she accompanied a ninety-year-old congregant who was dying. As her condition deteriorated, the congregant chose to discontinue any medical care except pain relief. In describing her own experience, Pat recalls:

Here in Berks County, families are closely knit and seldom move far from the place of their birth. Each day, one of her three daughters took a twenty-four-hour shift. They had families and they worked, but the two who were not on duty stopped by every day, faithfully caring for their mother. It just broke my heart, because I was never close to my mother due to her mental illness and substance abuse. It was difficult at times to be part of this environment of devotion, but I was also healed by the relationship. I visited two to three times a week, prayed with the mother and her daughters, and witnessed the love they shared.

During the final day of her congregant's life, Pat celebrated communion in the kitchen with eight members of the woman's family, most of whom hadn't been in church for years. According to Pat, it was a holy moment. "There were tears, and there was church. You see, church can occur anywhere, even in a kitchen." Pat observes, "God heals us as pastors when we're trying to provide Christ's love and healing to others." Pat experiences God's presence flowing through her to others as she carries out her vocation as pastor to the sick and dying. But Pat also recognizes that she receives as well as gives, even though her intent is always to focus on her congregants' needs.

Like Robin, Pat is honored to be with people in holy moments of death and grief, when God's love is made visible in intimate and healthy family relationships. "In that kitchen as we shared communion, God was present in ways that you could see, feel, touch, and taste!" Sean, an Evangelical Lutheran Church in America pastor in Southern California, admits that one of his great inspirations in ministry, "despite the dysfunctional relationships I regularly observe, is the great love ordinary people have for one another and the devotion of friends and family to their chronically ill relatives and companions." Time after time, I have heard pastors give thanks for the opportunities to stand with others on holy ground, where *chronos* and *kairos*—clock time and God's time—penetrate each other, creating a "thin place" through which God is revealed in everyday life.

When I spoke with Faith, a United Methodist pastor whose congregation is near the Chesapeake Bay, she had recently learned that her mother, who has been facing cancer for several years, had just a few months longer to live. The mother of two young children, Faith admitted that her initial response was immediately to brave the snow and catch the first plane to Florida, where her parents live. But after a few moments of prayerfully centering, she realized that the best initial response for all parties concerned was "not to panic but wait and see." This same calm intentionality is reflected in Faith's ministry with the dying, despite the challenges she may be facing personally. Nevertheless, Faith admits that she was not eager to do her first funeral at her current congregation. When she arrived at her new appointment at this town-and-country church, a fifty-nine-year-old congregant was already dying. Faith confesses that because of her mother's life-threatening cancer, she "didn't want to get too close." On the day her congregant was transferred to hospice, with just a few days to live, Faith recalls that she requested an anointing. "I anointed her hands, head, and feet in gratitude for her life. The family and I touched and massaged her, a practice that I had learned at CPE." Her congregant died on Faith's mother's birthday. Faith recollects, "Waiting for her to die was like waiting for a baby to be born. It was an amazing mystery. She died as we gathered around her reciting the Lord's Prayer."

Most new pastors admit that the death they most dread is that of a young person due to a car accident or terminal illness. Diane, a Disciples of Christ pastor from Indiana, arrived at her first congregation shortly after an eight-year-old was diagnosed with life-threatening cancer. Diane admits, "This was tough, since I had an eight-year-old niece who I spoiled rotten. I couldn't imagine her having cancer and dying so young."

But despite her anxiety, Diane faithfully ministered to the eight-year-old and her family. "I tried to keep an open heart, but most days after I saw her I went home and cried. My heart broke every time I saw her. But this young child had great faith. She wanted a funeral celebration because she knew God would be welcoming her in heaven." To be faithful to her calling and to respond to her own emotional needs, Diane sought out a trusted counselor, who "allowed me to process my feelings, tears and anger, in a safe place." She also sought out a wise older pastor who helped her with her prayer life and self-care. "I couldn't have done this alone," Diane affirms. "My counselor, a seasoned pastor, and my husband got me through. The funeral was heart-wrenching, but it was also a celebration of life, of a beautiful child who was welcomed into the loving arms of God."

Unresolved grief can shape the lives of people, congregations, and small towns. One evening, Wanda, whom I introduced earlier in this chapter, missed a turn in the road on her way to visit a congregant. As she circled past the church, she noticed a man walking in the parking lot beside the church. She explains, "When I asked if I could be of help, he told me that his uncle died in a propane truck explosion on the church grounds fifty years before. As we talked, we discovered that in the fifty years, including immediately after the explosion, there had been no public worship service acknowledging the community's loss, which had included a number of firefighters who had come to the scene of the accident." The community had been torn apart by grief nearly three generations earlier but had never gathered as one to share its common loss of eleven of its citizens.

Wanda asserts that this providential encounter was a "God thing." She began to organize a community memorial service, including people who remembered the event, the fire company that had lost firefighters in the explosion, and survivors of the town tragedy. More than two hundred people attended, only thirty of whom came from her church. In the wake of the service, the church received sufficient gifts to create a memorial

garden near the site of the accident to commemorate the tragedy and honor the deaths.

The Teaching Pastor

The reality of death provides an opportunity for spiritual
transformation for the pastor and her or his congregation.
While death will always remain a mystery, awakening feelings
of both fear and hope, it provides opportunity to learn about
the deceased as well as prepare for our own deaths. Faith is a
storyteller, and she has found sharing stories an essential part
of her care for grieving families. In planning the funeral, she
takes time to ask questions about the deceased in a process one
of her mentors calls *naming*. She invites the family and close
friends to enter into the story, to share stories and details about
the deceased person's life, including her or his childhood, values, accomplishments, humorous and revelatory moments,
hobbies, and special family times. "I love to learn about the person, whether in conversation or by looking up their genealogy,"
Faith explains. In the conversation, Faith not only discovers important things about the deceased, she also opens the door for
family members to remember favorite moments, share untold
stories, and learn about new dimensions of their loved one's life.
In the communal storytelling, the bereaved family members often also learn new things about themselves and their relationships. In the spirit of feminist theologian Nelle Morton, Faith
"hears [family members] into speech."[1]

Karen sees teaching as an essential part of dealing with issues of death and dying. She often opens the door to reflection
on death when she is speaking with a seriously ill congregant or
her or his family. Like many other pastors, Karen believes that
preparing for death is essential to faithful living. Recently, she
brought a counselor from the local Samaritan Center to speak
with her congregation about faith and final decisions as a way

to help congregants spiritually prepare for death by reflecting on the whole of their life and preparing ethical wills.

Luke, a North Carolina United Methodist pastor, sees theological reflection on death and dying as an essential part of his ministry:

> With the current controversies surrounding end of life issues, I want my congregation to make decisions from a Christian perspective. I don't have a preconceived notion about the decisions people should make, but people need to prepare for the inevitable. If you believe in the resurrection and life everlasting, then death is not the ultimate evil. We can let go of life-support treatments, morally and spiritually. I remind my folks that there is a big difference between ending a useless medical treatment and killing someone. With all the misconceptions people have, I decided to have a series on death and dying. I spoke about death and everlasting life in the Bible but then invited an attorney in the church, the local funeral director, and a hospice nurse to share their perspectives.

In the wake of seven deaths in her first twelve weeks of ministry, Wanda knew she had to do something in response to the grief that pervaded her congregation. When a member invited Wanda to accompany her to a grief support group at another church in the area, Wanda discovered that her congregation also had a new mission in providing support for bereaved people. While the other congregation's group was helpful in many ways, each session, Wanda recalls, "presented a very conservative theological perspective and ended with an altar call." Shortly thereafter, Wanda sponsored a Blue Christmas Service at her congregation, which offered an opportunity for attendees to acknowledge and share their experiences of loss in a liturgical context. Wanda also felt called to initiate a more open-spirited Grief Share Group in her own congregation. In addition, Wanda knew that she needed to address the needs of children in the congregation. In the course of teaching the confirmation class, she took the confirmands to the local funeral home, where they had an opportunity to visit every room, including the embalming room, and to engage in dialogue with the funeral director. Wanda notes, "In small towns, funeral directors are a resource for congregational death education." As a small town boy myself, I concur with Wanda's recognition that in villages, funeral directors often have an intimate relationship with the deceased and their families. They go to church together, belong to civic organizations, bowl and play golf together, and meet each other at grocery and hardware stores. Most small town funeral directors want to support pastors and help them in their care for the deceased and their families. Contrary to public perceptions, most funeral directors, whether in small towns or urban areas, see their work as a ministry to people in need.

Professional Growth in Responding to Death and Bereavement

Despite its universality, death is something we never entirely get used to. It breaks our hearts and often shakes our faith. The reality of death opens up questions in areas as diverse as spirituality, human destiny, healing, grief, and unfinished family business. In pastoral ministry, people experiencing death, serious illness, or bereavement are at their most vulnerable but also most open to hearing the good news of Christian hope and resurrection life. Therefore, new pastors must grow in their ability to respond creatively to death and bereavement as pastors, shepherds, and theologians.

Most new pastors, like Jackie, Paul, and Jennifer, cite the importance of clinical pastoral education in helping them face the realities of death and suffering in a pastorally sensitive way. Today, many denominations require CPE, or its equivalent, as part of preparation for ministry. Still, pastors, like other professionals, need to keep up on their death education. Many seminaries and counseling agencies provide ongoing theological education in issues such as depression and suicide, caring for the dying, and bereavement care. These workshops serve as opportunities for new pastors to share their emerging wisdom and experience as well as learn from more experienced pastors and counselors. They often help create a network of counselors to whom pastors may refer congregants and provide a way to get to know other local resource people, such as funeral directors and leaders or members of support groups.

While the cultural dynamics may differ between small towns and big cities, pastors need to get to know the local funeral directors. When he is able, Matt, a pastor in the Washington, DC area, goes to the funeral home with his congregants. Going to the funeral home enables Matt to get to know family members who have come from a distance and to gather information that will help him weave together personal and theological reflections in his funeral homily. Occasionally, he serves as a resource for bereaved family members in making decisions about caskets and other aspects of the funeral. Wise pastors, especially those of smaller urban and rural congregations, recognize that funerals are important to the well-being of their faith community, where most members have known most of the deceased and their families for many years. More than a few new pastors have formed death education partnerships with funeral directors and local counselors that enable congregants to reflect theologically on issues such as end-of-life care, planning the funeral service in advance, and choosing between burial and cremation.

Most mainline pastors recognize that they need to develop a theology of death. In contrast to their more conservative colleagues, they seldom have clearly defined images of the afterlife or see human destiny in the stark contrast of heaven and hell. While I believe that a dose of humility is essential as pastors face the mysteries of God and human existence, we can still provide biblically grounded images of hope, both in the funeral service and in our personal counseling with families. While resurrection rightly will remain a mystery to mortals, pastors can claim that the Christian faith is a resurrection faith and that God's love embodied in the life, death, and resurrection of Jesus is stronger than death. We can share our affirmations of divine grace and forgiveness without specifying the mechanics of salvation and healing.

Most new pastors soon discover that the reality of illness opens the door for theological reflection on prayer and miracles. Therefore, pastors need to think about how their images of God shape their understanding of the power of prayer and the natural order of life. I believe that this should be done through the pastor's teaching and preaching ministry, but prior to that in the solitude of the pastor's own theological reflection. As pastors who are called to pray at the bedside and graveside and to lead intercessory prayers in public worship, we are challenged to ask ourselves questions such as:

+ Does prayer change things? And, if so, what difference do our prayers make in health and illness?
+ Does prayer change God's mind? Or has everything already been decided in advance by God's eternal decree?
+ Does prayer open the door for God to be more active in the world? Is God more effective in transforming our lives as a result of our prayers?
+ Does God act supernaturally, violating the laws of nature to save some but apparently not others? Or does God always act within natural processes?

Most pastors cite the significance of colleagues and mentors in helping them learn how to respond creatively to issues of death and dying. Jen remembers how important it was for her to share her first two funerals with more experienced pastors, who affirmed her role while providing guidance in funeral planning and care for the family. Jen affirms gratefully that she still uses a version of a liturgical template that a more experienced pastor provided.

As stated throughout this book, ministry is a relational profession that can deplete a pastor's spiritual and emotional reserves, especially when we respond to death and grief in our congregations. More experienced pastors, as well as colleague groups, can serve as resources for new pastors who are developing a theology of death and finding healthy ways to respond to the death of congregants. New pastors, and pastors at every stage of ministry, need to constantly monitor their levels of stress and emotional well-being. Like regular blood pressure screening, emotional and stress level monitoring enables new pastors to remain emotionally available and physically well in order to respond faithfully to their congregants' pain and grief.

Creative Wisdom for Ministry in Death and Dying

As pastors, we are, to use the language of the apostle Paul, ambassadors for Christ, teaching and healing in Christ's place. Nowhere is our role as God's embodied presence more essential than in times of tragedy, death, and vulnerability, whether in the wake of the attacks of September 11, 2001; in our response to a drawn-out dying process; or following a car accident that kills three teenagers.

While we can never fully prepare for unexpected tragedy, we can deepen our own spiritual resources so that we will be a faithful presence amid the struggle. Following the example of Jesus during a storm at sea, we can be quietly present in the boat when the waves crash all around us, waiting for the right time to minister to the fears of our congregants. Even if the waves don't immediately cease, our own sense of God's presence amid the storms of life assures our congregants, in the words of Julian of Norwich, that "all will be well and all will be well and all manner of things will be well." Pastors provide spiritual comfort best when they combine spiritual disciplines with self-awareness.

First, we need to cultivate a deep personal relationship with God through prayer and contemplation. Regular times of stillness awaken the quiet center from which all insight emerges. In addition, the practice of breath prayer, intentionally opening ourselves to God's Spirit by breathing slowly and deeply, especially in challenging situations, calms, centers, and creates a space for nonanxious pastoral care. Many pastors have noted that, when walking from the car to the hospital room or the home of a grieving family, they take a few extra steps and deep breaths to deepen their sense of God's presence and the confidence that God will guide the conversation.

Second, we need to be mindful of how our own death experiences shape not only our attitudes toward death but also our ministry to the dying and the bereaved. Those firsthand experiences can make us aware of our vulnerabilities and of situations in which we become emotionally detached when we need to be pastorally present. It goes without saying that if we find some deep unresolved grief or difficulty being emotionally present around dying people, we should seek out a wise pastoral care giver or spiritual director. Take some time to reflect on or write about the following questions:

+ What was my first experience of death? How did the people around me respond? What were my feelings? In what ways, if any, does this experience still shape my responses to death?
+ What was my most challenging encounter with death and dying? What were my feelings? In what ways, if any, has it shaped my responses to death?
+ What are my feelings about the reality of death? How do I feel about my own death? Who is the person whose death would be most heart-wrenching to me?

+ Which congregant's death would be most difficult for me to face and respond to?

+ What are my feelings about the afterlife? How do they shape my ministry? Do I have a theology of the afterlife?

+ Have I put into place a living will or advance directives regarding my medical care if I am unable to make decisions myself?

+ If I am a parent, have I nominated people to be guardians for my children if I die before they are eighteen years old?

+ Do I have life insurance to provide for close family members if I predecease them?

+ What would I like in my own funeral or memorial service? Would I like to be buried or cremated?

Faithfully responding to these questions and making a commitment to self-monitoring will enable you as a pastor to be more emotionally present and theologically helpful in responding to dying and grieving people. The questions will also begin to alert you to your own stressors and suggest ways you can avoid burnout and compassion fatigue.

CHAPTER 8

THE SPIRITUAL LIVES OF SPIRITUAL LEADERS

Rejoice in the Lord always; again I will say, Rejoice. Let your gentleness be known to everyone. The Lord is near. Do not worry about anything, but in everything by prayer and supplication with thanksgiving let your requests be made known to God. And the peace of God, which surpasses all understanding, will guard your hearts and your minds in Christ Jesus.

Finally, beloved, whatever is true, whatever is honorable, whatever is just, whatever is pure, whatever is pleasing, whatever is commendable, if there is any excellence and if there anything worthy of praise, think about these things. Keep on doing the things that you have learned and received and heard and seen in me, and the God of peace will be with you.

—PHILIPPIANS 4:4–9

THE BIBLICAL NARRATIVES DESCRIBE THE ADVENTURES OF people and communities whose lives were transformed by their encounters with the living God. While not all pastors can point to transformational experiences of God like those of Moses, Jeremiah, Isaiah, Mary of Nazareth, Mary of Magdala, Peter, or Paul, every pastor has experienced the movements of God in her or his call to ministry. These are the moments when we see the world with new eyes, discover God's vision for our lives, or experience new insights to respond to challenging situations. Like Moses coming down from Mount Sinai or Jesus after his transfiguration, we come down from the mountaintop with new perspectives on our ministries and greater energies for healing and transforming the congregations we serve.

If we people, as the apostle Paul says, live, move, and have our being in God's presence, then everyone, whether clergy or lay, is guided by God at some deep level. I believe that God seeks abundant life for all creation and that God's call to abundance comes through moments of inspiration, guidance, discernment, ecstasy, healing, and peace.

The God who called us, subtly or dramatically, to ordained ministry continues to call pastors each day to fulfill their roles as spiritual leaders, prophets, and priests whose vocation is to enable the church to fulfill its own unique calling for this time and place. While God's call is always graceful and precedes our efforts, vital ministry emerges in an ongoing process of call and response in which God's call addresses each person in her or his unique circumstances, including personality type, environment, life situation and religious history, and previous responses to divine inspiration. Our openness to God's call through spiritual practices awakens us to deeper dimensions of divine activity in our lives and ministries.

The spiritual practices that Paul counsels in Philippians 4:4–9 find their context in Paul's affirmation that "the one who began a good work among you will bring it to completion by the day of Jesus Christ" (Phil. 1:6). "The harvest of righteousness" (Phil. 1:11) God intends for our lives and ministries is, in the spirit of Paul's horticultural image, the result of cultivating a sense of God's dynamic and graceful presence through ongoing spiritual practices. The cultivation of our spiritual lives as pastors is essential to our healthy congregational and institutional leadership. In Paul's words, we are to "work out your own salvation with fear and trembling." Yet, we are never alone, for

God is always providing us with the gifts, grace, and encounters that will deepen our spiritual lives—"for it is God who is at work in you, enabling you both to will and to work for [God's] good pleasure" (Phil. 2:12b–13). Spiritual practices always emerge from and are supported by God's grace, even when we must work hard to maintain our spiritual disciplines amid the many varied and demanding tasks of ministry.

Most new pastors struggle to maintain healthy and consistent spiritual disciplines. Yet, it is clear that the ability of the pastor, as the community's spiritual leader, to nurture vital spirituality in his or her congregation is intimately connected to an interest in and experience of God's movements in his or her own professional and personal life. Further, spiritually committed pastors are more likely to possess greater resources that can be tapped to address the spiritual yearnings of their congregants through preaching, spiritual direction, and group leadership.

Many Paths to Pastoral Spirituality

The spiritual journey for each pastor reflects the uniqueness of his or her life and situation in ministry. Natalya, a United Methodist pastor in Tower City, Pennsylvania, recognizes that keeping a spiritual discipline is essential for maintaining vitality and inspiration in her preaching and pastoral leadership. A graduate of Wesley Theological Seminary, Natalya was, prior to entering seminary, one of my student leaders in the Protestant campus ministry at Georgetown University. During my tenure as her university pastor, I observed Natalya's sense of God's call toward ordained ministry grow from initial questioning and contemplation to a clear sense that God was calling her to a ministry of congregational transformation within the United Methodist Church. In response to her growing gifts and self-awareness, I gave her ample opportunities to preach at university chapel, lead retreats, and take program leadership roles in the Protestant campus ministry. Evangelical in spirit and intellectually curious, Natalya embodies the best of the Wesleyan tradition of warm-hearted missional outreach.

Although practicing the discipline of morning prayer while carrying out her responsibilities as the mother of a toddler hasn't always been easy, Natalya asserts that she needs quiet time every morning in order to be a faithful pastor. At the heart of Natalya's spiritual practice are the three simple rules of John Wesley, as articulated by Bishop Rueben Job: (1) do no harm, (2) do good, and (3) stay in love with God.[1] Natalya notes that her primary practice for the past several years has been "to read the Upper Room daily disciplines and respond to the journal that goes with it." Since the readings often relate to passages from the lectionary, Natalya recognizes that the daily devotions "keep the lectionary alive for me." An English major in college, Natalya is tempted to be an ivory tower preacher, whose homiletical erudition might easily fly over the heads of her small town, primarily working-class congregation. While she still does her homiletical homework, reading commentaries and doing her own research on the lectionary passages, the daily lectionary-based devotional disciplines keep her, by her own admission, "grounded in my own lived experience of God's presence in my life and the lived experience of God moving in my congregation." As Natalya avers, daily prayer disciplines inspire a "personal, vital kindling of passion, helping me discern what the word says to me as a child of God, who also happens to be a pastor." In the years ahead, Natalya hopes to deepen her experience of God in her life and ministry by covenanting to spend time not only in the discipline of morning prayer but also in short but regular afternoon and evening times of prayer and reflection.

Karen, a Mennonite pastor in Lancaster, Pennsylvania, is a morning person. She wakes up each morning with "a pervasive sense of joy, a joy that persists even in the midst of congregational struggle." For Karen, like the apostle Paul, joy is not an accident but the result of a disciplined spirit. At least three mornings each week, Karen spends half an hour practicing *lectio divina* as she sits prayerfully in the presence of God. Karen recognizes that no spiritual leader can flourish in isolation. She regularly meets with a spiritual director, who keeps her focused on God's presence in her ministry. Karen's ability to claim her pastoral authority as a woman in a denomination that has often stood in the way of women's ordination has grown as a result of meeting with her spiritual director. "It has been essential for me to hear someone name in my life what the church needs."

Becky, a Church of the Brethren pastor, also cites the importance of spiritual direction in maintaining a vital and healthy ministry. Becky affirms, "Having a spiritual director enables me . . . to share in confidence about how God connects with my life and profession. It helps me to understand where God is moving in my ministry as I seek to discern 'Where's God in all of this?'"

Not a morning person at all, Todd, an American Baptist pastor in Northern California, takes a few minutes each night to "pray for my family, congregation, and the world. I visualize God's love surrounding each one. I also take time to review the day, giving thanks for God-sightings in the course of the day and asking for forgiveness for sins of omission and commission." Many other pastors take a few minutes each night to practice their own version of the traditional *examination of conscience* as a way of recognizing God's presence throughout the day, confessing their shortcomings, and letting go of the past in preparation for a good night's sleep and the adventure of a new day.

David, a Presbyterian pastor and recovering alcoholic, also recognizes the importance of relationships in spiritual growth. Although he experiences solitude and the opportunity for spiritual reflection while he walks his dog, David maintains his spiritual life by "keeping up with my recovery and regularly meeting with my sponsor." In the midst of the challenges of seminary and his first congregational call, David attributes his ability to be "clean and sober" to healing relationships, accountability, and the support of his wife. For David and most new pastors, spiritual practices are not an escape from the concreteness of daily life but a response to the challenges and brokenness of ourselves as pastors and of our congregations.

No one type of spiritual practice is suitable for all new pastors. It is clear that the God who brings forth planetary, ethnic, and intergalactic diversity also affirms the diversity of human experience and spirituality. I believe that our spiritual practices emerge from the interplay of divine inspiration and our unique personality types and life situations. Our spiritual lives involve place as well as time. Like the Celtic spiritual guides, we may find a quiet center in the discovery of "thin places," holy spots where God's presence permeates our daily lives. Robin, the pastor of a town-and-country United Church of Christ congregation in Northwest Ohio, sees her kitchen as "a holy place in which her cooking becomes a spiritual activity." As she prepares meals for friends and family, Robin regularly has conversations with God. Contemplative cooking in the familiarity of her kitchen alleviates the stresses of day-to-day ministry and awakens her to the sense of the holy in everyday life.

Often spiritual disciplines have been the domain of introverts, who experience God in moments of contemplative prayer and quiet meditation. Many extroverts feel a sense of guilt and impotence at their inability to "be still, and know that I am God" (Ps. 46:10). An ENFP on the Myers-Briggs Type Indicator, Robin finds it difficult to pray in solitude. Her prayer life is profoundly relational and embodied in day-to-day encounters. In her quest for a consistent spiritual practice as well as healthy relationships beyond the church, Robin regularly attends a monthly meditation group in a nearby town. Robin describes her attendance as "an appointment I keep with myself, regardless of how busy the week may be." Twice each month she meets with a colleague in ministry for lunch and conversations about their spiritual lives and ministries. They have become spiritual directors or friends for each other, listening in prayerful confidence to each other's deepest yearnings for God.

Although she claims a growing sense of introversion since entering the ministry, Jackie confesses, "I fight against what ought to be my spiritual practices according to the traditional stereotypes of what it means to be spiritual. I'm not a person who is contemplative by nature. I'm just not going to spend thirty minutes a day in silent meditation." She finds her spiritual center in her thirty-minute commute to and from church morning and evening. Her car is her "moving monastery" in which she listens to inspirational music. On the journey to work, she prepares herself spiritually for the day ahead.

Jackie has also discovered the importance of physical movement as a spiritual practice. Often in the course of the afternoon, Jackie will go into the sanctuary of her church and, as she describes it, "walk around the sanctuary praying for people in the church." This not only connects Jackie with her congregation but also provides a rejuvenating spiritual break in the middle of her day.

A United Church of Christ pastor, Robin participates in her congregation's prayer shawl ministry. She moves her fingers in prayer, lifting up prayer concerns and intercessions for the people for whom she knits. Always handy with tools, Steve and Terri, a clergy couple from Northern California, experience God's presence in making toys for disadvantaged children and participating in their congregation's Habitat for Humanity mission. "We feel our connection to God and families we'll never meet as we make a dollhouse or help put up the roof on a Habitat project. We think of it as prayer with our hands. For us, it truly reflects our commitment to see Christ in the least of these."

A long distance runner and Episcopal priest, Joy prays as she runs through the woods adjacent to her Massachusetts parsonage. "In this quiet time, I pace myself with a spiritual word, or mantra, like *love* or *shalom,* for about twenty minutes, and then for the next twenty minutes, I visualize world situations and events in my family's life and in the congregation, and experience God present in the lives of those for whom I pray." In her daily spiritual discipline, Joy has integrated the stress-reducing relaxation response, promoted by regular ritualistic activities, deepening her relationship with God and maintaining her physical well-being. A midlife Presbyterian pastor, Mark no longer runs three miles a day; he walks each morning, after spending time with the lectionary readings for the week ahead. According to Mark,

> New ways of looking at Scripture come to me as I walk through my neighborhood. Writer's block disappears and I feel open to God's inspiration. Sometimes, I stop for a moment to write down my insights and then move ahead, enjoying my three-mile-an-hour pace and the sense of life that movement gives me. Often when I return from my walking meditation, the sermon is already written in my mind and the words flow as soon as I turn on my computer.

Eclectic Spirituality

Today, many pastors find inspiration in following an eclectic or interfaith approach to spiritual formation. A graduate of Pacific School of Religion now pastoring a congregation in Westminster, Maryland, Jennifer states, "My mornings are very important to me, and I do my best to protect them. My practices include reflecting on my dreams from the night before and what they may mean for my personal growth. I also spend time in spiritual centering." While Jennifer often reads the Gospels as part of her morning prayer, she also uses "angel cards" as a devotional discipline. According to Jennifer, "Each card describes a spiritual virtue and then provides a quotation reflecting on that particular virtue. I pick a card each morning as part of my personal discipline. I often pick the same card a few days in a row, and often the cards I pick highlight areas of spiritual growth. The cards support my goal of mindfulness in ministry." Jennifer's interest in angel cards and dream interpretation reflects the importance of synchronicity in a pastor's spiritual growth. Synchronicity, or meaningful coincidence, reminds us that God is giving us inspiration through the apparently ordinary and otherwise unnoticed events of our lives.

Jennifer also notes the intersection of health and spirituality in her disciplines. A student of reiki healing touch, a form of hands-on energy healing, Jen regularly participates in a reiki healing circle where she gives and receives reiki healing treatments from her colleagues in the group.[2] Jennifer's use of reiki as a spiritual discipline reminds pastors that we can never separate body and spirit. What calms the spirit calms the body, and what brings physical well-being also nurtures our spiritual lives. Jennifer's participation in the reiki healing circle reflects the importance of relationships in the spiritual formation of new pastors.

Tom also embraces an eclectic, interfaith spirituality. A graduate of Claremont School of Theology in California and a United Methodist pastor, Tom combines yoga and centering prayer in his daily discipline.

> After my morning cup of coffee and a quick look at e-mail, I close my eyes and focus on my breath and a specific prayer word for about fifteen minutes. Then I do a few yoga positions to energize and embody the quiet I've just experienced. Often after this time of quiet, gentle movement, I'm ready to read a religious classic for a few minutes before my family wakes up. I keep coming back to the Gospel of Mark, the *Tao Te Ching*, and Thomas Merton's *New Seeds of Contemplation*.

Given the growing spiritual eclecticism in American culture and Christianity, these pastors are pioneers in shaping a new kind of Christian spirituality that joins East and West and body and spirit. Many new pastors have opened the doors of their congregations to yoga and tai chi classes. Others sponsor conversations on world religions, health and healing, and emerging and missional Christianity. Their eclectic spiritualities enable them to respond creatively to the growing number of seekers who describe themselves as spiritual but not religious.

Creative Wisdom for Spiritual Practices

"Pray as you can, not as you can't" is the wise counsel of spiritual guides throughout the centuries. While books on spiritual formation often focus on practices like sitting meditation and contemplation that are often more accessible to introverted pastors, I believe that every pastor can find a practice that fits her particular gifts and graces, personality type, season of life, and ministerial situation. Pastors can practice God's presence, making sacred the present moment, through a variety of spiritual practices: sitting contemplation, walking prayer, prayerful jogging, kitchen mysticism, observing synchronous events, reiki and other forms of body prayer, and holy driving.

Many pastors need to find creative ways to take the first step in discerning an appropriate spiritual discipline. Others just need to explore a variety of techniques in order to find the one that resonates with their personality type or personal situation. There are a number of very good texts on spiritual disciplines that reflect the holistic and multidimensional approach of this book. I suggest the following texts as starting points for the adventure of finding a spiritual discipline:

Dorothy Bass, *Practicing Our Faith: A Way of Life for a Searching People*
Maxie Dunnam, *The Workbook of Living Prayer*
Bruce Epperly, *Holy Adventure: 41 Days of Audacious Living*
Bruce Epperly, *The Power of Affirmative Faith*

Bruce Epperly and Katherine Gould Epperly, *Tending to the Holy: The Practice of the Presence of God in Ministry*

Richard Foster, *Celebration of Discipline: The Path to Spiritual Growth*

Kent Ira Groff, *Active Spirituality: A Guide for Seekers and Ministers*

Gerald May, *The Awakened Heart*

Joyce Rupp, *The Cup of Our Life: A Guide for Spiritual Growth*

Marjorie J. Thompson, *Soul Feast: An Invitation to the Christian Spiritual Life*

I also invite new pastors to consider seeking regular spiritual direction. They can often find the names of spiritual directors by consulting their judicatory officials, contacting a spiritual center nearby, or looking online for resources at Spiritual Directors International (www.sdiworld.org). Spiritual direction involves an intimate one-on-one relationship. Therefore, it is very important to find a trained or wise spiritual director whose theology, personality, and spiritual orientation nurtures your own spiritual growth in dynamic and creative ways.

Kate Epperly and I provide a more detailed approach to a process of contemplative self-awareness, inspired by Gerald May, in *Tending to the Holy: The Practice of the Presence of God in Ministry*. This is one way a pastor can get in touch with her or his spiritual yearnings.[3] Begin by simply *pausing* in the course of your daily activities, turning off your computer, closing the door, switching off your cell phone, or going on a walk. When we pause, we open ourselves to intentionally *noticing* the quality of our experience. We may feel our stress level, note our physical condition, or discover for the first time the sound of a chirping bird singing outside of our study. We may find out how oblivious we are to the holiness of the present moment, incarnate in our bodies, emotions, thoughts, relationships, or environment. Like James Stewart in the Frank Capra classic, we may discover that, amid the challenging tasks of day-to-day ministry and personal life, we truly do have "a wonderful life."

In that moment of noticing, we take time to *open* ourselves to God's movements in the present moment by listening for the "sighs too deep for words" (Rom. 8:26) or an intuition leading us to the next step in our ministerial adventure. As we become open to God's presence, we allow our spirits to *yield and stretch* to embrace God's call in our lives. We might choose to take time to reflect on questions, such as: What new and creative thing is God inviting me to embody in my life and ministry? What larger vision awaits me if I let God move through my life? Arising from this time of centering, we can claim our role as partners in God's vision of shalom. We *respond* by exploring new possibilities for faithful excellence in our personal lives and ministries.

CHAPTER 9

THE HEALTHY PASTOR

Do you not know that your body is a temple of the Holy
Spirit within you, which you have from God, and that you
are not your own? For you were bought with a price; therefore glorify God in your body.

—1 Corinthians 6:19–20

John came to me with an air of hopelessness about
changing his lifestyle in a way that would improve his overall
well-being.

Do you remember my first year of seminary, how I put on the
"freshman fifteen"? Well, now that I'm in the parish, it isn't
any easier. It seems that from morning to night, I go from call
to call and meeting to meeting, and there's food everywhere.
Donuts in the morning at the office and pie in the afternoon,
when I'm visiting a parishioner! I've put on ten pounds in the
last three months, and it's not even Christmas yet! I used to
exercise, but now I get up, have breakfast with my family, and
hit the road on another day of ministry. I need to get control
of my life or I'll end up in the hospital. What can I do?

The story of this small town Presbyterian pastor could be repeated by hundreds of new pastors who once took their physical well-being for granted but have now discovered the occupational hazards of being a congregational pastor. Similar to members of the local police force, pastors seem to find pastry everywhere on their appointed rounds!

Finding a healthy diet is just one aspect well-being pastors must contend with as they seek to glorify God in their bodies. As Christian leaders, we are called to proclaim a deeply embodied faith in which the word becomes flesh (John 1:14) in our attentiveness to God's incarnate and creative wisdom. In my conversations with pastors at every stage of ministry, I have found that virtually all pastors struggle to maintain a healthy lifestyle amid the demands of ministry. How new pastors tend to their physical well-being may very well be tipping points in the overall health and success of their ministries as well as their own lives.

Like every other aspect of ministry, a minister's health is a spiritual and theological issue. Many pastors preach about grace but practice a theology of works-righteousness in which they seek salvation through the success of their efforts. Others speak of the body of Christ yet live solitary lives, with virtually no support from friends and colleagues. They think that they can go it alone without the companionship and prayers of a community of friends and pastoral colleagues.

Sadly, many pastors are "practical Gnostics" when it comes to self-care. They assume that if they are faithful to the many tasks of ministry, God will take care of their health. Yet, time after time, faithful ministers falter because they have treated their well-being as incidental to their fidelity as pastors. I have heard this common complaint repeated dozens of times: "I know I should take care of myself, but I just don't have time. I go from morning to night—between getting the kids ready for school and putting them to bed at night, household chores, and pastoring this congregation, I barely have time to see my husband much less take care of myself." This confession is reminiscent of words from the Song of Solomon: "They made me keeper of the vineyards, but my own vineyard I have not kept!" (1:6b).

In the course of the pastoral enrichment seminars at Lancaster Theological Seminary, I regularly invite new pastors to read Scripture in the spirit of *lectio divina*. I recall one group of new pastors who prayerfully contemplated the words of Mark 6:30–46. The passage begins with the return of the disciples after their first mission apart from their teacher, Jesus. After they report their success, Jesus invites them to "come away to a deserted place all by yourselves and rest a while." He recognizes their need for a physical sabbath, because "many were coming and going, and they had no leisure even to eat" (v. 31). I received a number of interesting responses from this group of high-functioning new pastors:

+ That sounds like me. I don't even stop to eat lunch some days, and if I do, I grab some fast food to stuff in my face while I'm checking e-mail.

+ I need someplace to get away from it all. I can't seem to escape the phone calls, e-mail, and voice mail. I'm sorry now that I gave the congregation my cell phone number. I wanted to be available. Now, I have nowhere to hide. Whenever the phone rings, I feel compelled to answer it.

+ Jesus just asks the disciples to go away for a while. He doesn't even tell them to pray. Sometimes I simply need downtime—pizza and beer with my husband or a nap in the middle of the afternoon.

+ Hmmm. I wonder if Jesus had compassion because he took a break from ministry. When I don't take a break, the people seem like a nuisance. It's like compassion fatigue. But when I'm rested, I'm able to respond with love and care.

+ It's interesting that the passage begins with Jesus taking time to get away and it ends, after feeding the five thousand, with Jesus sending his disciples away and going up to a mountain to pray.

✦ This is good news for me: it's OK to take a break in the middle of the day or go home to be with my kids or enjoy a matinee if the sermon's finished on a Wednesday afternoon.

As I said earlier, I believe many pastors suffer from a version of works-righteousness, the belief that they must somehow earn their salvation rather than trusting the presence of God's grace in their ministries. As one pastor admitted, "There just don't seem to be enough hours in the day. And, then, I think that if I just work a little harder, things will work out at the church—we'll turn the corner and finally grow in members." In forgetting that grace applies to the pastor, too, many new pastors think that they can go it alone and that the future of their congregations is entirely in their hands. In contrast, one of the themes of Matthew 6:30–46 is that good ministry is grounded in trusting God's graceful presence; that is, God's care for sparrows, lilies of the fields, and pastors alike. In a grace-filled, interdependent world, described in Paul's image of the body of Christ (1 Cor. 12), many gifts for ministry are present within each congregation and complement and support the gifts of the ordained minister. God is working through the events of our lives to provide the resources pastors need for faithful excellence in ministry. Therefore, it never ever fully depends on us. Like Jesus, we can trust God and others to take over when we need a break. We can take a holiday, leave unimportant tasks undone, delegate, and trust that "God will make a way where there is no way," in the spirit of African American wisdom, in our churches and pastoral ministries.

Time for God

While pastors cannot fully control their schedules, they can be intentional about their use of time, finding creative and dynamic rhythms of work, rest, study, personal time, and family life. The biblical tradition recognizes the importance of sabbath keeping as a spiritual practice that not only promotes one's relationship with God but also transforms one's experience of time. According to Scripture, even God keeps a sabbath. A divine sabbath may seem a perplexing theological concept in light of God's omnipresent creative and sustaining activity. I believe, however, that the divine sabbath suggests that rather than overfunctioning and intruding on creaturely freedom, God gives us room to freely create and to take responsibility for our role as God's companions in shaping the earth. Like the sabbath-keeping God, many pastors experience greater well-being when they let go of the need to be in control and open themselves to God's grace and inspiration working within the gifts and talents of their congregants.

Sadly, many pastors suffer from what physician Larry Dossey describes as "hurry sickness" or "time sickness" by overscheduling, working long hours without rest, and going from appointment to appointment and task to task without any criteria for distinguishing between the essential and inessential aspects of ministry. One of my former students, Jackie, the pastor of a midsized town-and-country church in Central Pennsylvania, is learning how monitoring her time contributes to greater joy and well-being in life and ministry. After completing a time study at the request of the lay leaders, Jackie discovered that she worked an average of fifty-four hours each week, not including the six or more hours she spends commuting back and forth between her home and the church. Using these findings Jackie created a more manageable schedule and now typically leaves for church after 9:00 a.m. after working at home for a couple of hours, a measure that cuts her commute from seventy to thirty-five minutes. Still, Jackie puts in a long day at the church and calling on congregants: she often arrives at church at 10:00 a.m. and seldom leaves before 6:00 p.m. on regular days, and 9:30 p.m. on evenings when she has meetings. Like many pastors, Jackie's days at home are filled with phone calls and sermon preparation. Jackie confesses, "A pastor's work is never done, and I often find it difficult to take a day off. And on weekdays, my goal is to work no more than twelve hours on a given day. I love being pastor of this church, but if I don't stop and take time off, I'll wear myself out."

One creative way Jackie has responded to her lenghty commute is to claim her automobile as a holy space. Jackie seldom practices sitting meditation but spends her drive praising God through song and prayer, focusing on God's presence in her life. Music is an essential part of Jackie's life, and she fills her iPod with songs that nurture her spirit. Jackie notes, "My spirituality goes with me in the car."

Jennifer, a graduate of Pacific School of Religion who pastors a town-and-country church in Westminster, Maryland, a rapidly growing suburb of Washington, DC and Baltimore, registers time stress as "pain in my neck." That pain tells her that she is stressing out and not taking enough time for prayer, rest, and meditation. An INFP, Jennifer recognizes the need for a rhythm of rest and work, solitude and community, in her schedule. Jennifer says, "I am at my best when, after a long and busy day, I schedule the following day with only a handful of activities." Jennifer has transformed time by choosing to take a "silent Friday," in the spirit of Mahatma Gandhi. While she is flexible about her Fridays and responds to church emergencies when they arise, she typically maintains silence until 6:00 p.m. Friday evening. While her husband, whose office is at home, initially found her silence throughout the day problematic, he now chooses to answer her phone on quiet days and looks forward to the breaking of silence at supper.

Finding time for stillness and sabbath is especially difficult for parents of young children. Tom, a United Methodist pastor in a rural Maryland village, is grateful that the parsonage is next door to the church. "On the whole, people respect my privacy. What is good is that I can come home throughout the day to be with my wife and children. When my wife goes to work three days a week, I spend part of the day just playing with the three- and the five-year-old. If the secretary needs me, she gives a call, and the kids and I come over. The kids can play in my study if I need to work on something there." Tom admits that with two small children and a working spouse

> My days are filled from morning to night. Right now, I pray on the fly or as I look at my children's faces. When I have too much of church or the kids, my wife and I go out to dinner and a movie. We're blessed with a number of good babysitters in the neighborhood, and we don't hesitate to use them. Somehow, just playing with the kids or going out to dinner or a movie puts my schedule in perspective. If I take care of my relationships, I discover that I always have enough time for the tasks of ministry.

A pastor's schedule is unpredictable. An unexpected death or medical emergency can turn a pastor's week upside down. Therefore, wise new pastors plan their downtime for rest, family, and sermon and worship preparation. Eric, the pastor of a Disciples of Christ congregation in Missouri, does his best to "seize the day" for study and preparation: "I always try to begin my worship and sermon preparation on Monday morning, bright and early. I've found that just a few hours reflecting on the lectionary and choosing hymns starts the week off right. Even if something unexpected happens, I already feel partly prepared for Sunday morning. I still aim to preach a well-prepared sermon regardless of what happens during the week."

Mindfulness is the key to intentionality in the use of time. Jennifer notes physical signals that indicate when she is working too hard or taking her work too seriously. Another pastor, Steve, knows that he must slow down when

> I start to feel busy. It's not a physical sensation as much as feeling burdened by too many things and feeling hurried from

morning to night. When I begin to feel this way, congregants become an interruption rather than a blessing. I've learned that when I begin to feel really busy in my gut, I need to look at my schedule to see if I can reschedule or cancel an optional meeting and go home for a few hours just to watch a movie, read a book, or take a nap.

Tempted to hit the ground running after a busy Christmas week, Steve recognized the telltale signs of busyness and spent the Sunday afternoon following Christmas watching a Sherlock Holmes marathon and then, on Monday and Tuesday, going sledding with his kids, reading the latest Sue Grafton mystery, and going out for dinner with his wife. "When I returned to the church Wednesday afternoon, I felt refreshed and looked forward to an afternoon of hospital visits and sermon preparation."

While most pastors have difficulty making sharp distinctions between their personal lives and pastoral lives, those who are intentional about living a balanced and healthy life tend to experience time as a friend rather than an enemy. Although our response to time varies from week to week and according to our personality type and family obligations, healthy ministry involves intentionality in shaping our schedules. Healthy pastors tend to practice some of the following behaviors:

1. Taking time for a full day off every week for play and rejuvenation. If ministerial emergencies make taking a day off difficult particular weeks, find other times for relaxation and relationships, or take two days off the next week.

2. Planning sermons and worship during low-demand periods, often charting sermon topics and worship services weeks in advance.

3. Making a commitment to *sacred space* and *sacred time* by practicing a sabbath for prayer and reflection on ei-

ther a weekly or a daily basis. If you can't take a full day each week, I suggest finding a few hours for quiet reflection, study, or prayer as a reminder that all time is God's time.

4. Balancing quiet days with busy days if possible by not scheduling two appointment-filled days in succession.
5. Looking regularly at one's calendar, marking in advance sabbaths, days off, and study and preparation times, and sticking to this schedule unless an emergency arises.
6. Learning to say no on occasion to activities that are peripheral to the church's mission and the pastor's own mission.

Every pastor experiences periods of compassion fatigue in the course of dealing with the traumatic experiences of congregants and the anticipated and unanticipated demands of ministry. Brownout and even burnout are possibilities in every ministerial career. However, intentional practices of transforming time through prayer, meditation, relationships, and letting go can open us to God's abundant *kairos* time in the midst of ever-flowing *chronos*.

Stress and the Spirit

Some days are just "go, go, go, go," notes Jeff, the pastor of a small but growing United Methodist congregation in Tulsa, Oklahoma. Jeff is one of my "Timothys," having been, like Natalya, one of my student leaders in the late 1990s when I served as Protestant chaplain at Georgetown University. A passionate, mission-oriented alum of Duke Divinity School, now in his fourth year in ministry and the father of a newborn, Jeff works hard to keep balance in his life. "Some days, like yesterday, begin with responding to an unexpected death of a church patriarch, and continue with a number of hospital visits and marriage counseling in the evening." Other days, Jeff admits, stress surfaces when "everyone is sweating the small stuff, and I'm working hard not to succumb to their anxiety." Jeff commented, as did a number of other pastors, "Being a solo pastor has its own built-in stresses. The weight of success or failure is often on your shoulders, especially when key people fail to do their jobs." According to many solo pastors, "The laypeople want you do everything, and you only have so many hours in a day to respond to their needs or pick up the pieces of jobs unfinished." Being a solo pastor is especially challenging when you want to spend both quantity and quality time at home with your spouse and child or children, or if you are single and you want to spend time with your family or close friends.

As the reflections of the previous section indicate, our attitudes toward time are pivotal: will the stresses of ministry lead to chronic, rather than occasional, distress and compassion fatigue? Like Jennifer, Jeff practices a Friday sabbath. He admits that his Friday sabbath is a type of boundary keeping for him. He does his best "not to do any church work, even sermon preparation, on Fridays. Sure, I mow the lawn and run errands, but for one day a week, unless there's an emergency, I focus on family life and self-care."

When he first came to his current congregation, Jeff asked his administrative assistant to tell any callers that he was taking a sabbath every Friday and that he would call them back the next day unless it was an emergency. His Friday sabbath keeping led to the following humorous pastoral exchange. A long-term member called regarding a sick relative who had been hospitalized. When his administrative assistant relayed Jeff's message to him, his response was, "I didn't know we had a Jewish preacher." Later that day, when Jeff took an hour away from his sabbath to visit the hospital, he was greeted by the man's relative with the salutation, "There's our new Jewish pastor!"

Because the tasks are often unrelenting in ministry, new pastors frequently need to take time out during the day to reduce their stress level. Jackie takes several deep breaths as she sits at her desk whenever she begins to feel anxious. Craig keeps a pair of running shoes, shorts, and a T-shirt in the closet of his study. Whenever the day gets too stressful, this Church of the Brethren pastor changes clothes and goes out for a jog. "In those thirty minutes on the road, I let go of the stresses of the day. I begin to feel relaxed and ready for the next challenge. I'm lucky, since the pastor's study has an adjoining bathroom with shower."

While each of us internalizes stress in different ways, chronic stress can lead to physical illness, burnout, and poor decision-making if pastors do not creatively respond to it. Our experience of stress—that is, how we respond to the expected and unexpected events of ministry, family life, social involvement, and personal nurture—is a matter of perspective. Jesus reminded his stressed-out disciples that the lilies of the field and the birds of the air neither toil nor spin but live fully in rhythms of God's grace. Despite the rigors of his own ministry with outcasts and traumatized people, and his frequent encounters with theological controversy, Jesus affirmed that God takes care of the smallest details, and God will take care of us. Here pastors need to practice what they preach. While we can't force ourselves to trust God with the details of ministry and relationships, we can, over time, begin to place all of the events of our lives, both small and large, in God's hands. If God's goal is to bring the good work of our ministry to fullness, then we can trust God to give us the resources to face the challenges of each day. Even on the most difficult days, we can remember, nothing can "separate us from the love God in Christ Jesus our Lord" (Rom. 8:39).

When the stresses of life become too great, pastors typically focus on the negative aspects of ministry. The problems we face become immense, and we see our resources as meager. At such times, going it alone is the last thing a pastor should do. When he is particularly stressed, Jeff not only shares the challenges of ministry with his wife but he also picks up the phone to call a "classmate from seminary and together we share the burdens of ministry as well as its joys."

While Jesus went to a quiet place to experience spiritual and physical replenishment, David, a Presbyterian pastor in Columbia, Pennsylvania, goes to a noisy place. A midlife "rocker," David put together a band after he received the call to an urban congregation. Playing lead or rhythm on one of his two Stratocaster guitars enables David to "let go of stress and enjoy the moment." Like a number of other pastors, David has discovered the no that says yes: "There are so many things to be done here and so many requests, but I've learned to say no so that I can do good ministry here, spend time with my wife, and have a life outside of church. I can't do everything, but I can do some things with great fidelity. Right now, I experience God's call in growing this church and increasing its outreach in its urban neighborhood. I have to put every other request in the background."

Jen, the associate pastor of a Metropolitan Community Church with congregations in Lancaster, York, and Reading, looks forward to springtime and the start of the baseball season each year. For Jen, going to the Reading Phillies' ballpark is the ultimate stress release and respite from the demands of ministry: "Baseball is the heart of my life. I can't wait for springtime to come each year. The ballpark is a sanctuary, somewhere I can go to leave the world behind. I enter the gates, and I'm really here, at the ballpark and nowhere else. During the game, I let everything go, there's nothing but the game. I live in the now."

Healthy ministry involves discovering one's own rhythm of prayer, rest, and work. God calls us to share our lives with others and to be willing to sacrifice as God's partners in healing the world. But ministerial stewardship also involves awakening to the ever-flowing streams of divine grace and healing that are available to us when we take time to pause and notice our well-being and discover the intimate relationship between caring for others and caring for ourselves.

Moving with God's Spirit

The biblical story tells of a people on the move. Our parents in the faith never had to worry about getting enough exercise. The children of Israel marched across the wilderness. Mary walked several miles to visit her relative Elizabeth. Jesus's life was a constant walkabout. In the history of ministry in North America, John Wesley's circuit riders traveled from town to town, and the first Disciples of Christ pastors preached on Sundays and farmed throughout the week. While occasionally gluttony might have been an issue for pastors in colonial and frontier days, our parents in the faith, unlike many of today's pastors, did not have to plan an exercise routine. For them, daily life was an ongoing physical adventure.

Often new pastors feel so overwhelmed by the challenges of their first congregational call that they give up exercising altogether. Yet, when she reflected on her excuses, Karen, a town-and-country Mennonite pastor, said, "I don't have time *not* to exercise, if I'm to remain a faithful and effective pastor." Her own quest for physical well-being has led her to join Curves, an exercise club that combines whole body exercise stations with a social element, as patrons move from one exercise station to the next. Karen notes, "I've not only improved my health but also made a few new friends as a result of my exercise program."

A small town Disciples pastor in Missouri, Sharon discovered one morning, as she struggled to climb upstairs, that she needed to take a hard look at her lifestyle. As she reflected on her daily life as a single pastor, she recalls, "I drove everywhere. I had left the city but still acted like a city dweller. Even though the market was just five blocks away and most of my local parishioners lived less than a mile from the parsonage, I hopped in my car without thinking. Most days I even drove the two blocks to the nursing home. The only time I really walked was when I cut across the lawn from the parsonage to the church building." Convicted by her lifestyle, Sharon decided to become a walking pastor, not unlike Paul, whose story is told in an earlier chapter. In preparation for changing her ministerial lifestyle, she drove around her town, marking distances from the church to the places she normally visited. She discovered that virtually all her pastoral tasks, with the exception of hospital visitation in the county seat several miles away and visits to the farm families living outside of town, were within a twenty-minute walk from the parsonage. "That day," Sharon remembers, "I decided that unless the weather was bad, I would do all my pastoral work on foot." Amazing things happened to Sharon's ministry when she began to do her ministry on foot. Townsfolk began to know her as the "walking preacher." Sometimes, they would even join her. More often they would wave as she went by or invite her to come up to the porch to "sit a spell" or have a glass of lemonade. "Much to my surprise," Sharon admits, "some of my best pastoral work came through 'accidental' encounters as I walked through town. Relieved of the pressure of an intimate and planned pastoral visit, people opened up to me as we walked to the grocery store or stopped in the city park." Sharon has discovered that her walking has not only improved her overall health, energy, and creativity but it has also been an opportunity for evangelism and congregational outreach that has paid off in visits from many of the people she has met on her peregrinations. Further, as an advocate of ecojustice, Sharon began to feel a greater congruence between her values and daily life. "I am leaving a smaller carbon footprint and also save nearly a tank of gas each month."

Determined to find a way to respond to the stresses of ministry, Martha, a small city pastor in Ohio, walks twice each week with another pastor. The two of them, one American Baptist, the other Church of the Brethren, joke about their "ecumenical walks." Martha notes, "Most days, we begin our four-mile walk talking about church things and blowing off steam. By the midpoint, we're simply enjoying the beauties of nature or laughing at the foibles of ourselves and our congregations." Walking helps these pastors creatively deal with the challenges of ministry emotionally, spiritually, and physically. "When I walk with my friend, I know that I'm not alone. I discover my problems are universal as well as unique. I don't have to take them home to my family. It seems like moving helps me let go of my problems and gain a new vantage point from which to do ministry."

Robin sees her commitment to physical well-being as essential to the credibility of her ministry. A second-career pastor, Robin asserts, "If I want my congregation to take health seriously, then I need to model healthy habits in my own life." Robin has chosen to literally walk the talk through regularly walking and doing Pilates exercises at home.

In the first few months of his suburban ministry, Josh admits that he "watched sports from his couch rather than participated in them." A lifelong athlete, with high school letters in basketball and tennis, Josh dusted off his shoes and racket and joined a tennis club. "Sure, it was a bit extravagant. But the cost influenced my discipline. Now, I play a few times a week, and so does my wife. We have both met new friends as a result of our membership." Back to his high school weight, Josh now joins a pick-up game of basketball with the United Methodist youth group: "They're surprised that an 'old guy'—almost thirty—can move this well. Our games after youth group meetings have created a bond among us. I've also gotten together with some of the other men in the church to play basketball once a week. Often what happens on the court spills over into off-court conversations about business, values, and faith."

Eucharistic Eating

What people eat and drink, according to the biblical tradition, reflects their relationship with God. Hebraic law saw the people's diet as a reflection of their faithfulness to God and an affirmation of their uniqueness as God's people. Jesus's ministry was characterized by radical hospitality, a common table in which people of all social classes were welcome. Even social outcasts, tax collectors, sinners, and people at the edges of religious propriety were welcome at Jesus's table. When the apostle Paul asserted, "'All things are lawful,' but not all things are beneficial" for Christians (1 Cor. 10:23), he challenged the behaviors of people who came early to agape meals and ate and drank more than their fair share. What we eat is a moral issue: it reflects both our stewardship of our bodies and our stewardship of planetary resources.

Becky, a Church of the Brethren pastor and a former seminary student, ate an omelet, made of Egg Beaters, as we talked about the challenges of authority and spirituality in ministry. When the topic moved to health and wholeness in ministry, Becky recalled that during a celebrative Alaskan cruise, she realized that she needed to lose weight. She decided that her first congregational call would provide an opportunity to change her lifestyle. She began to follow the South Beach Diet and lost twenty pounds in her quest not to be "another overweight pastor." Becky affirms, "God created a beautiful world, and I want to be beautiful too."

Jeff is discovering the importance of meals as a time for spiritual replenishment. For a long time, Jeff ate his meals at his desk, often checking e-mail and making phone calls between bites. Now, he leaves his desk at church each day to take an hour for lunch, even if it is 2:00 p.m. This creates a space for rest and rejuvenation in the middle of the day that enables him to be fully present for his next appointment.

Robin, a graduate of Eden Theological Seminary in St. Louis and in her first year of congregational ministry, asserts, "When your congregation loves you, they feed you." She continues, "My Italian background predisposes me toward a diet of fruits and vegetables as well as a love of cooking. The kitchen is a holy place for me, and I love to cook healthy food, purchased from the co-op or grown in my own garden." Still she recognizes that saying no to pastries is difficult, especially when they regularly show up on her parsonage doorstep across the street from the church or at her church study.

Robin believes that she is called to model health and wholeness for her congregation. Therefore, Robin has become mindful of both the quantity and the quality of what she eats. "Portion control is the key to healthy eating for me, along with a diet of organic food purchased from the local co-op." Robin regularly practices what my wife and I described as a "no thank you helping" at church potlucks; that is, she takes a small portion as a way of affirming the cook's efforts but also as a way of minimizing caloric intake. But eating is more than a mechanical process for her. Robin seeks to eat with a sense of gratitude as she remembers the people whose labor has made her meal possible as well as those who will be sharing dinner with her.

Sterling, who pastors a United Church of Christ congregation near Reading, Pennsylvania, is working on becoming more mindful about his eating habits. With his parsonage next door to the church, he recognizes that meals at home are important to him. He and his wife, Sue, now a seminary student, try to eat dinner together on a regular basis. Like me, Sterling faces the spare tire proportions of midlife. In response, Sterling has discovered that lunches at home are healthier, better tasting, and more economical than eating out.

Pastors can eat eucharistically, with a sense of gratitude for the blessings of both good food and the efforts of those who bring food to their tables. They can also give thanks for the gift and call to take care of their bodies so that they can minister with energy and care. Self-care is not optional in achieving faithful excellence in ministry, whether it involves days off or healthy meals. It is simply our grateful response to God's creative wisdom moving in our lives and all creation.

Creative Wisdom for Healthy Ministry

Caring for our physical well-being is an act of stewardship. All good gifts come through the creative wisdom of God; in caring for God's creation—whether the planet, our congregation, or our bodies—we are saying thank you to our creator. We are also claiming our role as God's companions in healing the world, first in our own bodies and then in our communities and the world.

Throughout this chapter, I have reflected on the importance of theology and spiritual practice in healthy ministry. The biblical tradition recognizes the importance of sacrificial living, but it grounds our sacrifices in trust in God's gracious presence. Therefore, let the Bible be your guide to healthy living in ministry. I invite you to read the following passages in the spirit of *lectio divina*.

1. After a time of quiet centering, read the passage slowly, letting the words and their meaning for you sink in without attempting to analyze the text.
2. Take some quiet time to rest in God's presence in the text.
3. Read the passage again, once again letting the words and their meaning for you sink in without attempting to analyze the text.
4. Take some quiet time to listen for the words and images elicited by the text.
5. If one image or word is most meaningful, focus on that word, exploring its meaning for your life and how taking its message seriously might lead to personal and professional transformation.
6. After several minutes, ask for God's blessing and insight on ways to embody the wisdom of the passage.

In this spirit, I invite you to reflect on Exodus 18:13–27, describing Moses's father-in-law Jethro's advice to Moses regarding the nature of leadership, and Matthew 6:25–34, Jesus's invitation to his followers to "consider the lilies."

Throughout the week, take time to read these passages. In what ways do they challenge your current approach to ministry? Where might you make changes in order to be a healthier pastor?

If you notice that these scriptures call you to change certain aspects of your ministry, what small steps can you take right now to transform your health and ministerial practice? Begin with one small but transformational step that will bring greater well-being and energy to your current ministry.

CHAPTER 10

RELATIONSHIPS MATTER

But Ruth said [to Naomi], "Do not press me to leave you or to turn back from following you! Where you go, I will go; Where you lodge, I will lodge; your people shall me my people, and your God my God."

—RUTH 1:16

THROUGHOUT THIS BOOK, I HAVE ASSERTED THAT PASTORS have many vocations. God calls pastors to be spiritual leaders of congregations and other religious communities, but God also calls pastors to experience holiness as friends, parents, spouses, children, volunteers, citizens, and creators. In this chapter, I invite you to focus primarily on intimate and holy relationships such as marriage and partnerships, parenting, and friendships.

Quantum physicists as well as process theologians recognize the wisdom of the Hebraic tradition and Paul's vision of the body of Christ (1 Cor. 12). We live in an interdependent universe in which our well-being depends on healthy relatedness. Whether we gain energy from relationships (extroversion) or times of quiet solitude (introversion), healthy ministry emerges from positive relationships both within and beyond the congregation.

Ministry, by nature, involves the whole of a person's life. Emergencies can happen at any moment, and the committed minister may have to leave the dinner table or postpone a day off. One phone call can transform what looked like a spacious schedule into a chaotic week of scrambling to respond to a tragic car accident or a natural disaster along with the necessary tasks of preaching, worship planning, and congregational administration. Family life is often disrupted, and sadly, many pastors forget their responsibilities to attend to their children and spouses as well as the troubled young adults and bereaved people in their congregations. Faithful excellence in ministry requires care for one's significant relationships beyond the church along with commitment to pastoral care within the church. Healthy relationships outside the church nurture and support the pastor's quest for ministerial excellence.

Monica describes herself as an introvert, prone toward being a workaholic. As pastor of both an established congregation and a new church start in Harrisburg, Pennsylvania, Monica admits that she has plenty on her pastoral plate. She was initially surprised when I contacted her about her relationships outside of seminary. Monica admits, "I thought I would fall into the *what not to do* model of ministry. The challenge when you have your office primarily at home is to avoid working from dawn to dusk. The challenge for me is learning to shut the door." As a single adult, Monica confesses that her love for ministry and the work she is doing is so great that she often needs the support of her family to say no to the many exciting tasks of ministry: "I think that my family, and especially my twenty-nine-year-old daughter, has been an essential call to balance. My daughter insists that we get together regularly. She reminds me when I don't give her the attention she needs in our relationship." Monica also avers, "Because I tend be more reserved, it suits me fine not to have a lot of relationships outside the church or the family. A lot of emotional energy is tapped in working at the two churches. As you can see, despite my external activity, I am very introverted. My energy is internal. I love people but I really need time by myself. When I close my door on my office, I choose to take time for sabbath." Monica is a good example of a pastor for whom rejuvenation is a matter not of establishing more relationships beyond the church but of taking more time for prayer, solitude, and reflection. Monica comments, "I love my churches, and I love what I'm doing, but I rejoice when I come home each day to a quiet home and time for rest and reflection."

Another pastor, Darryl, states, "I can't separate my ministry from relationships and family life. When I go home to Philadelphia, I'm always asked to pray at family meals. I'm a pastor wherever I go." Still, this single, Hispanic pastor finds a life outside his downtown Reading, Pennsylvania, congregation. Staying connected with his family keeps Darryl in balance. "I visit my mother in Philadelphia every weekend." Darryl is also active in sporting activities, "Once a week, I play soccer for the police department team." Darryl notes that his congregation worries about him burning out. Darryl reports that some members recently "told me to slow down and take time to play soccer even during Lent." Darryl recalls that when he first began dating his girlfriend of nearly two years, "My congregation was being very protective of me, wanting to make sure she was a good companion. They were excited about the relationship, and mothered me in my relationship."

While Darryl and Monica are content with their current status as single pastors, I would be remiss if I did not briefly note some of the challenges of being single in ministry. An introvert by personality type, Michelle asserts, "I like the quiet time for study and hiking in the woods that bound the manse, but sometimes it's lonely out here. I would love to have a companion nearby [with whom] to talk about theology and go out to dinner. I'm thinking about submitting my ministerial profile to churches in metropolitan areas next time." The single mother of two elementary-school children, Susan laments that she hasn't had a date in two years. "It's not easy dating as a single parent, but add the title of minister, that scares most men away." Daniel states that "Some people think being a single, male pastor is a dream, but frankly it's been a nightmare for me. Everyone in the church wants to set me up with their single niece or grand-daughter. I can't date in the church, and if I meet someone at a party or dinner, just mentioning I'm a pastor often stops the conversation." The pathway for single pastors isn't always easy; for better or worse, often they find their closest companions, including spouses and partners, among ministerial colleagues. Most learn that happiness in ministry, whether married or single, is a spiritual as well as relational issue.

Marty, a recent seminary graduate currently navigating a cross-country marriage, notes: "My biggest challenge in minis-try is not working too much. I try to take one day off a week, but two would be better in order to get a good rhythm of ministry and personal life. I am grateful for three seminary friends who live in the area." She is also learning to take advantage of the resources of the local seminary. Although she loves her church and is committed to serving God, Marty is learning early in her ministry that healthy ministry requires the interplay of work and play, activity and sabbath, focus and rest.

The Call of Extended Family

Cheryl, the pastor of a two-church charge in Central Penn-sylvania, sees grandparenting as a key vocation in her life. Her working children often need a backup babysitter, and each Fri-day is her "day with the kids." When I asked her about being a grandparent, Cheryl enthusiastically responded, "The grand-children are the joy of our lives. I do a lot of babysitting. Some-times I babysit as often as parts of four days each week. I can do this because my churches are small and I only work 'half time.'" Like many other small church pastors, Cheryl works out of the house and, in her case, shares some of the babysitting

with her husband, a college professor. Given the responsibilities of church and childcare, Cheryl admits that "because of the
grandchildren, trying to take a day off or study day is a challenge. I prepare my sermons when the kids are napping. My
husband and I go to the symphony each month, and that's our
special time together."

Betsy, a Mennonite pastor in Denver, Colorado, said that
her call to local church ministry involved commitment to her
family as well as the congregation. Her siblings and father live
in Colorado. Moving across country, Betsy shares, "allowed me
to be closer to family and especially support my aging father."
Betsy's husband was able to secure a position in global econom-
ic development work with a Denver-based organization.

Family was a key element in Steve's acceptance of the call
to serve a United Church of Christ congregation in the Boston, Massachusetts, area. A married, second-career pastor,
Steve states, "Our son and his wife were having a baby. I knew
that as a professional couple, starting out in life, they would
need extra support. When the opportunity emerged for me to
move to Boston, my wife and I were elated. She was able to
find a position in her field. Now that the baby's here, we spell
the kids with babysitting when they're worn out and usually
come over one evening a week so that they can have some time
together." A high-energy pastor who often has trouble leaving
church behind, Steve has discovered that his new vocation as
grandparent helps him to be a more attentive husband, parent,
grandparent, and, much to his surprise, pastor: "I used to work
nonstop when I was younger. I missed out on many special moments in our son's life. Now, when I see my grandson, I'm living
in the now. That's a big theological and personal change for me.
I'm learning to leave the future in God's hands and let go of
control along the way. I'm happier and more effective in ministry because of my grandparenting."

The pastor of a union congregation, Evangelical Lutheran Church in America and United Church of Christ, Sara

typically works at home, due to the lack of a study at church. Sara reports that her husband and she have forged a healthy ministerial partnership: "When I went to seminary, I quit working as the administrator for the local district attorney's office. After I was called to the church, Gary and I decided that he would stay home and help take care of our grandchildren during the day. Although we live on less money these days, we believe that somehow God will make this work."

Because the church doesn't have a study, Sara has created one on the lower level of their home. "Most days," Sara notes, "I'm at home till early afternoon. I do my sermon preparation, newsletter, and church business downstairs most mornings and surface a few times each morning and for lunch to be with Gary and the grandkids." For Sara, the best time for working and writing is in the morning. Unlike some pastors, Sara typically doesn't take a regular day of the week off but rotates her day off throughout the month. Her advice to pastors is to "be flexible. What works one month might not work the next. I don't take a particular day off. It just hasn't worked." Her congregation supports her flexibility and gives her plenty of time to be with family, spend time with her husband, and play golf.

The Call of Marriage with Children

Nate, a thirty-year-old United Church of Christ pastor in Central Pennsylvania, says that everything changed with the birth of their baby. He has learned the meaning of sacred time and space. Like me, Nate grew up a preacher's kid and confesses, "I thought I'd never be a pastor. But I discovered there's more for me to be as a person in the church. Here I can make a real difference in people's lives." Still, Nate had to overcome some hurdles, especially the tendency of pastors to be workaholics, as he considered the call to congregational ministry. Although Nate respects and loves his father, he admits, "I'm learning from my own childhood how to be a good parent. I grew up a PK [preacher's kid], and sometimes my dad was at church too

much. At times the church seemed more important than marriage and family. When I began ministry, I realized I needed to
make family a priority." Therefore, Nate always takes Mondays
off to be with his young son. He makes a point of taking every
afternoon from 4:00 p.m. to 7:00 p.m., except in the case of
pastoral emergencies, to spend time with his wife and child.
In his attempt to balance fidelity to ministry and family, Nate
asserts, "I take advantage of my flexible schedule to care for my
family. Now that I'm a father, I recognize that I need to get my
work done on time. I can't take it home with me as much I used
to before the baby came."

Nate reflects a healthy *ecology of ministry*. Good ministerial
leadership involves attending appropriately to the whole of a
person's life. Being an effective spiritual leader is difficult if you
are an absentee parent or partner or fail to attend to physical,
emotional, and spiritual well-being.

Mark, another United Church of Christ pastor in Central
Pennsylvania and, at the time of this writing, soon to be the
father of a third child, affirms that rituals are essential for integrating healthy ministry and family life. He has created what he
calls a transitional ritual. In Mark's words, "I meet my daughter
at the school bus stop at 4:00 p.m. Just to wind down, I leave
church at 3:30 p.m. and have a cup of coffee or a take a short
walk before meeting her. Unless there's an emergency, I make it
a point to have family time between 4:00 and 6:30 p.m." Like
many pastors, Mark's weeknights are filled with meetings, but
he takes time each evening to be with his wife: "Between 9:00
and 10:30 p.m. is our time." Mark has arranged to take several
weeks off for paternity leave following the birth of his third
child. As he notes, "Fathers need time with their babies too!"

Beth, a United Methodist pastor in her seventh month of
ministry, shared the joys and challenges of claiming family life as
a vocation along with ordained ministry. On the day we spoke,
Beth and virtually everyone else in Central Pennsylvania, including me, had been snowed in for the previous two days. She
happily reported that, once the roads had been cleared, "both

of my kids are having a sleepover, and I'm planning a night out with my husband." Like many new pastors, Beth admits that it is "difficult to let go of my ministry when I come home at night. Ministry can take up every waking hour if you let it. I am blessed that I have a spiritual director who helps me sort out my priorities."

Trying to be intentional about time is central as Beth seeks to balance ministry and family. Although she tries to take one full day and another half day off each week, she constantly asks herself, "How do I do errands and be a pastor and care for my family?" Beth is grateful to have a husband who "gets it." Beth reflects, "My husband and I had been in conversation both before and during seminary about what ministry would be like, and this prepared us to be flexible." Like many clergy families, scheduling is a challenge for Beth and her husband. When her husband and children are free on weekends, Beth is often busy with the responsibilities of ministry—weddings, final sermon preparation, and Sunday afternoon congregational and denominational programs. Raised in a fairly traditional family in which the roles of husband and wife were well defined, Beth admits that she is learning to let go of traditional roles in order to balance ministry and family life. One of Beth's first challenges came when she realized, She could not do it all. "Now, I take Fridays off and want to volunteer at my children's school. But, when would I clean house? It was a big deal for me to hire a cleaning lady to do work that had previously defined my marital role!" Beth further redefined her marriage roles when as she admits, "I had to realize that I didn't have to go to the grocery store. This doesn't make me less of a wife if I don't go to the store." Now, Beth's husband regularly goes shopping. Small changes can make a big difference in ministry.

Beth, like many pastors, has learned to negotiate things like funerals so that she can do things like go to her children's weekend sporting events. Beth recalls how she suggested an alternative time for a funeral so that she could support her children, and much to her surprise the family agreed. One of the hardest learnings for new pastors is that they also have a voice in setting the schedule for funerals and weddings. These events are only set in stone if the pastor forfeits her or his role in determining the shape of her or his ministry.

Beth is grateful for her husband's partnership in ministry. Although he is active in church, "it's not a package deal. He supports my work and sees it as important as his own." Mary, an associate pastor in a suburban Houston Presbyterian congregation, is also thankful for her husband's affirmation that "ministry is a call for the whole family." Her husband's positive experience as a PK enables him to "understand the challenges of my work and joining ministry and family life. We are spiritually growing together!"

Ronnette, another midcareer United Church of Christ minister, affirms that boundaries have been essential for preserving a healthy balance among marriage, ministry, and family life. Her life as pastor is complicated by the fact that her husband is town manager of the township in which the church is located. From the start of her ministry, Ronnette made it clear that "church was church, and township was township." She recalls telling the church leadership, "What goes on in the township can't go on in church. I'm not here to defend the township or my husband's work. If you have a problem, take it up with my husband at the township office. I can't be his messenger or secretary." For the most part, Ronnette's congregants have come to appreciate the wisdom of boundary setting and have recognized the importance of respecting her and her husband's professional boundaries.

The mother of two boys, one in elementary and the other in middle school, Ronnette describes herself as an "overachiever who is growing in her ability to let go of the need to do it all, for the sake of her health and her family's well-being." Today, rather than multitasking and juggling one thing after the other, Ronnette has learned the wisdom of doing one thing at a time.

She admits that this approach is "monumental, and reflects a transformation in my personal and spiritual life. At seminary, I was at everyone's beck and call. I was getting a lot done, but I wasn't happy." Nowadays, Ronnette's weekly calendar has two nonnegotiable appointments. "Monday morning," Ronnette states, "I set aside for prayer and meditation, and on Wednesday evenings we have family night for games and being together." In keeping good boundaries, Ronnette has integrated the inner and outer journeys of ministry and family life in a way that nourishes her spirit and responds to the needs of her children, husband, and congregation.

Jen, the associate pastor of a Metropolitan Community Church in Lancaster, Pennsylvania, confesses, "Church can consume you. It's difficult to manage your schedule and have family time when you're starting new things." Therefore, Jen and her partner Maria are intentional about regularly taking time to be together. Jen notes, "Maria and I set a regular date night. Sometimes it has to be a moveable thing, although we aim at Friday nights. We have to be together to sustain our relationship. When we have better conversations on the phone than in person, we need to find some real time together."

Tony, an African American pastor serving a small town, primarily white congregation, takes time to "get away at least once a month with my wife. Small town life can be a fishbowl, where everyone seems to be watching you. We go to a hotel to have time together and renew our relationship."

Clergy Couples

Over the past two decades, a growing number of couples have met in seminary and then pursued their vocations as partners in ministry, whether they share ministry in the same congregation or serve separate congregational charges. For more than thirty years, my wife, Kate, and I have been partners in ministry, parenting, writing, retreat leadership, and consulting.

While our first attempt at cominsitry nearly thirty years ago was challenging due to our ministerial context and relational maturity, until 2010 we shared leadership of a small congregation in Lancaster, Pennsylvania. Like the clergy couples I will describe in the following paragraphs, we have experienced the great joys and challenges of clergy couples and are especially grateful for the opportunities that ministerial flexibility has given us for parenting and travel.

Matt and Becky are United Church of Christ pastors, serving in Mercersburg, Pennsylvania, and Hagerstown, Maryland, respectively. While Matt serves as solo pastor of a small town church, adjoining the historic Mercersburg Academy, Becky is associate pastor of a downtown congregation twenty miles away from their manse in Mercersburg. Over lunch at a Mercersburg bistro, Becky and Matt report that one of the greatest joys of being a clergy couple is that "you never lack for sermon material. We have our own clergy lectionary group right at home. When one of us is stuck on our message, we talk it over and usually discover new insights in the text." A key element of integrating their partnership in life and in ministry is professional understanding. As Becky says, "We 'get' each other's profession. We understand the emergency calls that take one of us away from home. When one of us has to leave at the drop of a hat, the other knows why and understands." Matt adds that this sense of partnership applies to their own family emergencies: "When our two-year-old daughter is sick and can't go to day care, we can usually rearrange our schedules." Matt and Becky agree that planning and flexibility are essential to successful ministry. They both make it a point to arrange their schedules so that one of them can always be with their daughter. Matt takes Mondays off because Mondays are Becky's main meeting day. Becky takes Wednesdays off so that Matt can go to meetings and make calls. Nevertheless, they still face many challenges in scheduling. Matt and Becky both noted, "Special services, like Easter and Christmas Eve, get complicated.

We have to juggle a bit or find people to help us out." They are grateful their congregations recognize that "it takes a village to raise a child" and often pitch in to support them.

I met with Jackie and Paul over breakfast in Rohrerstown, Pennsylvania. Like Matt and Becky, they appreciate their common vocation and see their ministry in separate congregations as a professional partnership in which they help one another out by showing up at special congregational events. Jackie and Paul, who met in seminary and whose marriage I had the honor to officiate, affirm, "While we work very differently, we share a common schedule and values." Like Becky and Matt, they recognize that "We're a built-in TextWeek.com. We ask each other, 'What are you preaching about? What do you see in the text?'" They also note the importance of sharing a common vocation, especially in emergencies: "When one of us gets the midnight phone call, the other doesn't complain, and knows, 'The next call may be mine'"

Over coffee in Claremont, California, Allison and Robert shared their ministerial journey. Like many other clergy couples, they met in seminary. Challenging for them is that they serve in two different denominations. Robert is United Methodist while Allison is Episcopalian. Robert explains, "We have the joy of an unspoken connection with our vocation. When I come home from a trying day of ministry or struggling spiritually with the lectionary texts, I know that Allison understands and supports me." Allison adds, "We take our mutual support for granted. Not all pastors are so fortunate to have a real companion in ministry." Learning together is essential to their professional and personal relationship. Allison affirms, "We experience a great deal of joy in working together in the Internet age. We're growing together as we learn about emerging Christianity and worship." They have also found their denominational differences helpful. Robert recognizes "the importance of a creative outside perspective from a different denominational tradition."

As associate pastors of large suburban congregations, Robert and Allison see their professional relationship as synergistic. "While we have our particular perspectives, we do homework together and share in our preparation. We are immersed in the same scriptures, although it often comes out totally different." Robert notes that having a companion in preaching and leadership often clarifies his own viewpoint. He states, "It has helped me in my preaching to have someone to share ideas with. Sometimes Allison asks provocative questions that change the course of my sermon, such as, 'Is that really your theology? How will that be heard in the congregation? Are the older members going to understand that quote from *The Simpsons*'?"

Their professional synergy includes event planning. Allison and Robert have been heavily involved in leading a program that brings together Episcopalian and United Methodist churches. They also regularly colead retreats involving both their congregations. They rejoice in the fact that "leading retreats together joins our youth groups and swells the participation from fifteen to thirty teenagers."

Bonnie, the pastor of United Church of Christ congregation, has the added joy and complexity of serving as the pastor of the church where her husband, Daryl, is the minister of music. (Daryl and I collaborate regularly in seminary worship and music programs and together have authored a book, *From a Mustard Seed: Enlivening Worship and Music in the Small Church*.) Like the clergy couples I have described in this section, Bonnie and Daryl experience the joys and challenges of partnership in ministry. Bonnie notes, "Although we enjoy working together and have a creative relationship, we have to be careful to create spaces where work is off-limits."

Bonnie affirms that working together has a real blessing. "My husband and I have different styles of work, but we still mirror each other in ministry. We are partners in ministry. We bring out the best in each other. He's the kind of companion with whom I can have a spiritual dialogue. We are together as a team, and our relationship is stronger for it!"

Still, Bonnie and Daryl recognize that the intersection of ministry and marriage has limits. Often one of them says to the other, "How about we don't talk about church tonight?" If things are really intense at church, they often agree to "wait till tomorrow to solve the problem." They are parents of adult children and also have one high school boy at home. Bonnie admits, "When things are busy at the church, we tell our son: things are busy now, but we'll spend more time together next week." With their shared personal and professional values, Bonnie and Daryl are "a tag team as parents." They take time for themselves and for parenting: "Virtually every day," Bonnie avers, "we spend the last hour of the evening together, talking, reading, or watching TV. Simply enjoying one another's company." Still, despite their commitment to quality as well as quantity in their family life, Bonnie humorously recounts that after one particularly busy week, she and Daryl asked each other, "Why does it take a snowstorm to take a day off work!"

Despite the obvious benefits for their relationships that clergy couples identify, they face challenges in their shared vocations. Virtually every clergy couple agreed with Matt and Becky's assessment that the "hardest thing is juggling schedules." As I noted earlier, special services such as Easter and Christmas or unexpected crises such as a death and hospitalization are reminders to clergy couples that they need to have a backup plan and support system. Despite the inherent flexibility of ministerial schedules, some events in ministry are simply nonnegotiable.

Nearly every clergy couple with whom I have spoken struggles with the search-and-call or appointment systems in their denominations. Jackie and Paul ponder, "What will we do if one of us is called to another congregation, which may require a move or a change in lifestyle?" Becky and Matt ask, "Will we be able to find churches in the same area?" The same challenge is present within United Methodist appointment system. While the denomination's appointment system has become more family friendly over the past decade, clergy couples still recognize that they are subject to denominational decisions that may radically disrupt their current living and relational situations. Robert says that within his United Methodist Conference, "there is always a remote possibility that I may be moved to a congregation in San Diego or Hawaii. It's in the back of our minds, and we continue to talk about it. We are open to possibilities and the movements of the Spirit. If such a move happens, it will call us to discern where God is leading us as a couple in ministry."

Commuting is a major issue for Robert and Allison. While Robert lives in a Santa Monica parsonage, a short bicycle ride from church, Allison's round-trip commute is between two and three hours. While Allison's senior pastor supports her working from home, commuting is a necessity four days a week. As a couple, Allison and Robert have had to respond creatively to the disparity of their commute times. Robert notes, "I have become the cook and the housekeeper. It was hard at first, but we've come to terms with the commute. It was tough for me at first to empathize, but now I do my best to equalize things by shopping and working around the house." Sundays are the roughest days for them individually and as a couple. Allison leaves for church at 6:30 a.m. and often doesn't return home until after youth group, nearly 9:00 p.m. Robert, on the other hand, has a four-hour break at home after church before the evening youth group.

Robert and Allison admit that the disparity in schedules has made it difficult for them to put down roots in Santa Monica, where they live. Allison recalls, "In seminary we had friends galore. Now that we're in a parsonage in a big city, we are having trouble finding friends in the neighborhood. Both of us have grieved the loss of our intentional seminary community." They have found the social networking vehicle Facebook to be a blessing in meeting new friends and reconnecting with old friends. Both admit, "The first six to nine months in ministry were difficult. If we didn't have Facebook to connect us with others, I don't know what we would have done." They have connected with a clergy couple in the area with whom they regularly take bike rides and share their ministerial adventures.

Virtually every clergy couple says that while they share common values, interests, and schedules, a big challenge is what Tom describes as "closing the door on church." Tom shares an associate ministry position with his wife, Ingrid, at a United Church of Christ congregation on the West Coast. He states that as a result of their coministy, "[We] see each other more, do things together, and can share perspectives on things going on in the church. Because we work with families and youth, we use our family as a laboratory for planning events at the church." Nevertheless, Tom recognizes that "we have different boundaries and understandings of relationships at work and home." An extrovert, Tom often shares church issues and ideas for programs at home, to which Ingrid often responds, "I'm not at work." Juggling his PhD studies and church work is a challenge for Tom. "I have the 'Get that done' syndrome, and when I get an idea late at night, it's fun to talk about it. But Ingrid is ready for bed by 11 p.m."

Ingrid concurs in her assessment of the good points and challenges of coministy: "Our coministy enables us to share each other's strengths, and this often improves what we're individually doing. Tom is a theoretical and abstract thinker, a theologian interested in big ideas. I like to make things happen at the concrete level. I help ground Tom's work, while he helps me with the big picture." On the other hand, being coministers in the same congregation has its challenges. Ingrid admits that work and home life often blend into one another. "Sometimes over the dinner table, we realize we're still talking about church issues, and we have to stop and remind ourselves that we're at home now and we need to just enjoy each other's company." Boundaries are always blurry in ministry, but this is especially so when pastors work together in ministry. Copastors need to be intentional about creating spaces where church and home life are separate from one another. Still, much can be gained for a life together in ministry. Kate and I have noted that, in more than thirty years of marriage and ministry, different personality types, especially the introvert-extrovert dynamic, provide both joy and challenge for clergy couples. When couples recognize their different gifts and ways of relating to the world, their unique approaches to life can be synergistic rather than adversarial.

Creative Wisdom for Couples in Ministry

Healthy and creative ministerial relationships take time and intentionality. Quality time, what Scripture describes as *kairos* time, the holy moments of life, is grounded in a commitment to quantity time, to simply being around for the everyday moments of marriage, parenting, and ministry. Time is our greatest gift to one another. Along with time comes the willingness to be attentive. In this exercise, I invite you to take some time to look at your week, asking yourself the following questions.

Of the 168 hours each week, how much time do I spend:

+ on church-related activities, whether at church, on the road, or at home?
+ cultivating my relationship with my spouse, partner, or significant other (if this pertains to your life)?
+ with my children (if this pertains to your life)?
+ in prayer and meditation?
+ in self-care and health-promoting activities?
+ with friends outside the congregation?
+ in activities and relationships outside the ministry?

To be get a sense of how you are spending your time, you might create a pie chart, noting the rough percentage of time you spend on the above activities.

In this exercise, I invite you to join meditation with visualization. Begin in a comfortable position, breathing deeply and opening to divine wisdom. After a few moments, visualize the most important people in your life—for example, spouse, partner, friend, child or children, parent(s), grandparent(s), grandchild or grandchildren, friend, or mentor. Take a moment to visualize each one, noting that person's uniqueness, beauty, and gifts. In the quiet, pray for each one, and ask for God's wisdom in responding to their needs and deepening your relationships with them. After going over the list prayerfully, take time to thank God for each one and for the gift of relationships.

CHAPTER II

ASSOCIATE MINISTRY
AS A CREATIVE
CHALLENGE

Now there are varieties of gifts, but the same Spirit; and
there are varieties of services, but the same Lord; and there
are varieties of activities, but it is the same God who activates all of them in everyone. To each is given the manifestation of the Spirit for the common good.

—1 CORINTHIANS 12:4–7

OVER LATTES AT THE CHESTNUT HILL CAFE IN LANCASTER,
Pennsylvania, Kathy, a successful associate pastor of one of
the flagship United Church of Christ congregations in Central Pennsylvania, reflected on the nature of associate ministry:
"It's not a marriage, but it takes commitment and flexibility to
do well in associate ministry. You can't tell it's working until
you've been doing it awhile. Like a marriage, you never fully
know what you're getting into, but you need to work at it, getting to know one another's strengths and weaknesses and never
making the other one look bad in public."

For many new seminary graduates, their first congregational call is as an associate in a multiple-staff ministry. Like all

ministerial calls, being an associate pastor can be a source of growth, joy, and challenge. In this chapter, a number of associate pastors will share the landscape of associate ministry—the benefits, challenges, and best practices for associate ministers.

The Joys of Being an Associate

Over lunch at a suburban Baltimore restaurant, I met with three pastors, each of whom has served as an associate minister. One had recently been called to serve as a solo pastor in a nearby town. Their comments reinforced conversations I have had with associate pastors across North America. I asked what they saw as the benefits of an associate ministry.

- June, who had just moved from being a solo pastor to becoming associate pastor of a downtown church noted, "I like having a team and not being alone in ministry. While there's more freedom in being a solo pastor, I don't have to be 'on' all the time now. The spotlight's on the senior pastor and not me."
- Sandra, who had recently moved from an associate to a solo pastorate, echoed June's comments. "Now I'm the one who's on all the time. Before, I could stay in the background." Still, Sandra is glad for her new role as solo pastor. "I wanted to feel competent and make my own decisions in the church."
- Diana, now in her sixth month of ministry and the parent of an infant, affirmed the benefits of being an associate pastor. "It's good not to make the final decisions and to have a chance to learn on the job. I've found it helpful to talk with a more experienced pastor, especially when issues come up."

In talking with more than a dozen associate pastors, I found that they confirmed that the transition from seminary to associate ministry was in many ways beneficial to their personal and professional lives. Kathy notes that being an associate in partnership with an experienced pastor "taught me a lot about ministry and myself. I've learned a lot about what to do and what not to do as a pastor." Monica, now a solo pastor, recognizes the importance of team, especially during times of personal crisis. "In a staff of multiple people, there are always colleagues to back me up. When my daughter was ill, I knew that the senior pastor and staff would cover for me." Diana comments on the importance of having an experienced and confident senior colleague: "As I began my ministry, the senior pastor protected me; she put on the brakes so I could do one thing at a time and gradually grow in ministerial competence and authority." Diana's senior colleague, a mother of grown children, knew the challenges of balancing ministry and family life and supported Diana's need for a flexible schedule. A hard worker, Diana is grateful for a colleague who helped her set personal and professional boundaries. "It's a blessing to be able to have a baby and then be able to care for him. My senior pastor takes parenting seriously. I can take my baby to the doctor or work at home when he's sick." Diana adds, "Sometimes I feel a little guilty about being away from church," but she is, nevertheless, grateful to have a colleague who sees ministry from a holistic perspective and recognizes that faithful excellence in ministry involves the whole of a pastor's life and not only the performance of specific ministerial tasks.

The Challenges of Being an Associate

Virtually every associate pastor with whom I have spoken, from novice to veteran, describes her or his relationship with the senior staff pastor in the language of a 2009 movie: "It's complicated." While most associate pastors generally have good relationships with their senior colleague and peers on the church staff, they all recognize that the opportunities for misunderstanding, competition, triangulation, and conflict are many. As in a good friendship or marriage, there are moments when pastoral colleagues step on each other's toes, disregard the other's professional role, or neglect to communicate. As most associate pastors asserted, "Like a marriage or holy union, regardless of the promises you both make, you never quite know how it will work until you're finally living together."

Naomi, now a solo pastor of an American Baptist church in Connecticut, recalls that when she was called to serve as associate pastor for a one-year term, the senior pastor was inexperienced in multiple-staff leadership. Naomi notes, "From the very beginning, he was competitive and defensive. Any success I received threatened his sense of authority in the church. In subtle ways, probably even unconscious ways, he undermined my leadership and authority in the church." Sadly, he did not recognize the wisdom of 1 Corinthians 12:26: "If one member suffers, all suffer together with it; if one member is honored, all rejoice together with it."

Although Susan, now a solo pastor of a United Methodist church in the Baltimore area, has positive memories of being an associate pastor, one aspect of the senior pastor's style always grated on her. She remembers, "I don't think he was ever competitive or defensive. But often I had an idea—for example, a youth group work camp or worship service—that initially he saw as peripheral to his responsibilities. But when the programs became interesting or successful, he wanted to get involved and often took over. This often limited what I could do." Other associates report that, after spending hours crafting a worship service, they would show up on Sunday morning and discover everything had been changed. As one associate notes, "I was so angry, I could barely worship that morning. He acted as if there was nothing unusual in what he did. He assumed that he knew best and could make changes without consulting with me." These challenges point out the relational nature of multiple-staff ministry and the challenge for senior and associate pastors to communicate clearly and regularly regarding roles and expectations. "I know," Tom admits, "that despite her attempt at being egalitarian, she's still the head of staff, and I need to yield to her decisions."

In every family, triangulation, or the pitting of two parties against each other by a third party, is always a temptation. As congregational systems theory posits, triangulation is a way of lessening anxiety among members of a family or congregation by placing the blame or minimizing the accomplishments of a third party, usually the most powerful or most vulnerable member of the system. Multiple-staff ministries are no exceptions to the realities of relational triangulation. As "second chair" leaders, associate pastors are challenged to remain neutral in regard to criticism of the senior pastor or polarization between themselves and their senior colleague. Of course, senior pastors need to practice the same supportive neutrality in relationship to associates. Triangulation often occurs when a congregant compares the associate favorably with her senior colleague. "I am always pleased," Amy confesses, "when someone shares their appreciation of a sermon or my job performance. I thank them for their affirmation but always find a way to affirm him as well." Echoing Kathy's earlier comment about never wanting to make her colleague look bad, Kathleen, a Presbyterian associate pastor in North Carolina, states, "I simply keep quiet when they criticize the senior pastor." In describing his positive relationship with his senior pastor, Paul, a United Methodist associate in upstate New York, says, "My senior pastor and I always try to keep a united front at meetings and when congregational decisions are made. Even if we have different positions, I don't second-guess her in public, nor does she undermine my positions." Unity does not mean uniformity. Senior pastors and associate pastors have unique personality types, theological perspectives, and approaches to their ministries that need to be honored and affirmed in appropriate contexts.

Like parents in a family, associate and senior pastors need to protect as well as trust one another. The last straw for Cheryl, who left her call as an associate to become the pastor of new church start, was when the senior pastor let her take the blame for a decision he had authorized.

> When my grandmother was gravely ill, he told me to go back home for the weekend, and that he would take care of Sunday worship. When I returned and the chair of the board blew up at me for taking unauthorized leave, the senior pastor hung me out to dry. I knew that he was too frightened by the church's power dynamics to support me in any meaningful way. But from then on, I lost confidence and trust in his leadership and support. I knew I had to go. I put my ministerial profile out the next week.

While senior pastors need to trust the competence and good intentions of associates, they must also make every effort to stand by the associate pastors when they are criticized. Sadly, Cheryl's head of staff failed to realize that with authority comes responsibility and that ultimately the buck stops with the senior pastor.

Most associate pastors recognize that being "second chair" exacts a cost, and that is freedom to fully determine one's agenda in ministry. While associates on the whole appreciate not being the final authority in church business or the primary lightning rod for congregational controversies, they often lament the limitations placed on their initiative. Leigh Ann, an associate pastor of a large United Methodist Church in San Diego, California, affirms, "While I can't imagine a better situation for an associate, a place where I can work out of my strengths and passions, there is a built-in lack of autonomy. I have to fit into his vision." For Leigh Ann, being an associate is a spiritual discipline. "Your relationship is key to partnership in ministry. You need to figure out the nature of the relationship, and you also need to be humble. You need to recognize that you have something to learn from him [or her]." Although Leigh Ann has autonomy and a staff that reports to her as leader of one of the congregation's ministries, she also recognizes that she needs to be mindful of the senior pastor's approach to ministry. "I need to echo and fit into his vision of the big picture."

Kathy has come to realize that often when the senior pastor "says *we*, it also means me, and I have to work out my ministry in terms of his priorities." While most senior pastors seek to be egalitarian, their authority and role as head of staff both supports and limits the freedom of associate pastors. As one United Church of Christ pastor, a female working under the supervision of a female senior pastor, adds:

> I have a glass ceiling here in terms of what I can do. I can only do as much as I'm given permission. If I'm thinking of pushing a limit or moving in a new direction in my work, I need to consult with the senior pastor. I don't mind this too much, since I've come to realize that everything I do has an impact, large or small, on her work. I don't want to put her in the position of having to defend what I'm doing or blindside her by taking initiative where it hasn't been given.

Reflecting the apostle Paul's image of the body of Christ, senior and associate pastors need to be accountable to one another. What they do and how they relate to one another—and to other associates in a multiple-staff ministry—contributes to the overall well-being of the congregation.

Associate pastors also state that personality type and work styles can be a source of both joy and challenge. In an ideal situation, senior and associate pastors complement each other's gifts and personalities or have enough maturity to deal with their unique personalities, but such complementary ministry takes time and self-awareness. It also takes communication. Carolyn, the associate pastor of a Unitarian Universalist church on the Eastern seaboard, notes:

My senior pastor is laid back, while I tend to be a workaholic. I've definitely mellowed since working with him, and I've discovered that good ministry happens even when some details are left undecided. But there are still times when I need to put on my brakes in order not to push him faster than he wants to go. I will say, however, that he is now quite consciously trying to mirror my approach and explain in greater detail his plans and time frame. This makes me feel more secure and minimizes my anxiety.

Another well-prepared associate pastor gives a less sanguine account of collegial work styles.

I don't know how anything gets done around here. Everything, even worship planning, is at the last moment. Most of the time, I get a call or e-mail on Saturday night letting me know what's going on at our morning services. Other times, he gives me my assignments for the worship service just a few minutes before the processional. It drives me crazy. I like him, and he's generally good to work with, and he gives me a lot of freedom. But I need more lead time to feel secure.

Still, another associate pastor recognizes that she has learned a good deal from her partner in ministry: "His graceful style and sense that God will take care of things seems too laid-back at times for me. But in the process of working with him, I have reflected on my own tendencies toward being a workaholic. I am learning little by little to trust that things will be all right and let go of my need to be in control.

Getting to know one another's personality type is a key element in promoting collegial ministry. In describing her relationship with her senior colleague, Sandy notes:

I'm an ENFP in the Myers-Briggs, while he's an INFJ. We work together well and share a lot in common. But I know that he gets a little nervous at my more freewheeling, making-it-up-as-I-go-along approach, and I've learned not to bring an important issue to him after a big meeting or the morning services. He needs downtime, and I need to be patient. We've learned our own signals, and because of his respect, we've learned to joke about our differences and find some common ground that almost suits us both.

Seniors and associates alike need to be mindful of one another's unique personalities and gifts. Difference is the womb of possibility and the source of synergy, whether in aesthetic contrast, religious pluralism, or approach to ministry. When colleagues deal creatively and appropriately with differing visions, approaches to work, personality types, and theological perspectives, often a synergy emerges that adds to the energy and effectiveness of their congregational leadership.

Most associates recognize that at times they and their senior colleague will have different visions of where the church should be going. In most congregations, the senior pastor is charged with being the congregation's visionary leader. Ideally speaking, a congregation's vision emerges from the interplay of the congregants and their pastors, with the pastors working prayerfully together to craft the congregational vision. Still, once the vision is crafted, associate pastors need to recognize the senior pastor's role as the primary visionary leader within the congregation. When visions differ among the ministerial staff, most of the associates with whom I spoke said that differences need to be aired in private rather than in public.

While there are many other joys and challenges of being an associate pastor, I would be remiss if I did not bring in the issue of gender, a reality that enters into every senior and associate relationship, no matter the role, gender, or sexual orientation of each person.

While most pastors handle differences in gender and sexual identity with care and appropriateness, such differences need to be taken seriously by senior and associate pastors as well as pastoral relations committees. Female associates may need to differentiate themselves with care and directness when more patriarchal senior pastors or insensitive congregants ask them to perform tasks that they would not request of male pastors. Mutual respect and trust are essential in creative and effective collegial ministry, and this trust and respect begins when who we are in our giftedness and uniqueness is affirmed.

Relationship Is Everything

In her reflections on the similarity of multiple-staff ministries to marriage and other intimate relationships, Kathy asserts that "being an associate ministry is like marriage—but I didn't choose my partner." Whether the call to congregational ministry involves a search-and-call process or an appointment process, few associates and senior pastors have a long courtship prior to working together; often they are strangers who learn to trust, respect, and care for one another. Like any healthy professional relationship, intentionality is everything in multiple-staff ministries. Good senior and associate minister relationships don't happen by accident but as a result of carefully chosen ongoing commitments to working together in creative ways. In this section, I will share a few best practices from associate ministers, with the recognition that good professional relationships involve a high degree of mutuality. Over the years, I have heard the most effective senior pastors and heads of staff make similar affirmations about how they can most creatively respond to their ministerial colleagues.

SEEING THE BEST IN ONE ANOTHER

"It all begins with perception," notes Michelle, an associate pastor in the Pacific Northwest. "My perceptions of myself and my colleague in ministry make all the difference in the world.

Do I see him as a rival or a partner? Do I get beyond my defensiveness and knee-jerk responses and see him as a child of
God, trying to be faithful to his calling? But it's also about my
perception of myself. Do I affirm my gifts and value as a child
of God? Am I willing to be responsible for my behavior and
grow personally and professionally?"

Anyone who has been in a close relationship knows that our
judgments about others reflect our own experiences as much as
the reality of the other. Although I believe that each moment
provides an opportunity for creative transformation, it is clear
that our past experiences with parents and other authority figures; approaches to conflict and decision making; and personality types shape how we view others' behaviors. Another West
coast pastor confesses, "When I'm upset at my senior pastor, I
ask myself, 'Is it him or me?' If sin is a reality that shapes our
lives, then I have to admit that some of my interpretations may
be wrong. When I catch myself projecting my reality on a particular situation, I have to step back and try to see things from
his perspective as well as my own."

Recognizing that our experiences of others reflect who we
are as much as they represent the other's intentions has led
many associate—and senior—pastors to enter into spiritual
direction or therapy as a way of promoting healthy collegial relationships. "When I realized that my anger at the senior pastor
was really about my anger at my father and brothers, and other
male authority figures, I sought out a therapist," Jill confesses. "I
wanted a healthy professional relationship with give and take,
based on our intentions and behaviors, and not past history."
Todd discovered that he needed to explore his relationship
with the women in his life and explore his patriarchal assump-
tions when he found himself uncomfortable being supervised
by a female senior pastor.

Part of an associate pastor's commitment to seeing the
divine in her or his senior colleague involves an awareness of
the colleague's gifts and personality type, and a willingness to

respond in a complementary way to the senior pastor's unique giftedness. Of course, senior pastors need to be attentive to associates' gifts and personality types as well.

During his tenure as an associate pastor in Allentown, Pennsylvania, Mark remembers that he "got to know the senior pastor's gifts and how they intersected with my own gifts." Sandra recalls a similar dynamic from her own ministry:

> Once I realized we had very different personality types, I could be intentional in working with him. Knowing that he was a P [on the Myers-Briggs Type Indicator] and prone to make decisions in real time as he was verbalizing them, I learned to let go of my need to have him prepare weeks in advance. We often joked about our respective styles—I was a J who needed structure—and learned to meet each other in the middle. He even started putting together his liturgies on Thursday—rather than Friday—just so I could get some lead time. I believe we both grew as a result of honoring our different personality types.

While seeing God's presence in our colleagues may not always alter their behavior or lead to stress-free relationships, it enables us to let go of unnecessary relational baggage so that we can experience our colleagues as they are and assume the best, rather than the worst, in their behavior. We may still have to address differing viewpoints about ministry and theology, unconscious behavior patterns, or sins of commission or omission, but our approach will be grounded in affirmation and care rather than alienation.

Creative Communication

In looking back on her three-year experience as associate pastor of a Central Pennsylvania congregation, Monica notes, "Communication was essential in our relationship. When I wasn't making a point of regular communication with my senior pastor, things didn't go as well." In her case, Monica needed to ini-tiate regular conversations with the senior pastor. This was all the more essential because her study was on a different floor from the senior pastor's, and unless she made a point of stop-ping by, they might go a few days without any interaction.

Mark asserts that evaluation and communication go to-gether. "I needed to know how he thought I was doing and what I was supposed to do in certain situations." Diana sees communication as a way for associates to share their needs and perceptions as well. "Communication is everything. When we meet regularly, it gives me the opportunity to let the senior pas-tor know what I need to be good in my work as well as a part of the whole. Regular communication reminds me what's impor-tant to me in my life and ministry. It also lets the senior pastor know my priorities."

Regular communication serves as both a relational safety valve and an opportunity for clarification and midcourse cor-rection. On occasion, senior pastors inaccurately assume infor-mation has been conveyed to associates. Over time, ongoing lack of information leads to feelings of confusion, mistrust, and alienation. Some senior and associate pastors meet for a few minutes every few days just to go over current events and issues going on at the church as well as meet regularly for extended discussions every week or two.

Good communication requires intentionality. While per-sonality type and schedule affect the nature and timing of meetings, the most successful multiple-staff relationships in-volve the interplay of regular meeting times, informal chats in the hallway, dropping by to say hello, and longer retreats for vi-sioning and planning ahead. Regular meetings allow colleagues to promote a united front to their congregants without having to be uniform in approach. In my own work as a departmen-tal head of staff, I have learned that regular meetings with the team provide an opportunity for me to see our mutual work in new ways and to explore new possibilities in the ministry of theological education. When we focus on process as well as product in relationships, we often discover greater creativity and partnership. Good leadership, whether from the "first" or "second chair," involves the willingness to let go of agendas in order to be open to God's vision speaking through your colleague or the group synergy.

CLARITY IN JOB DESCRIPTION

Virtually every new pastor affirmed the importance of a clear sense of work responsibilities. All of them recognized that good ministry is fluid and flexible and at times, as one pastor recognizes, "you have to drop everything if there's emergency and you can't tell your senior colleague 'It's not my job.'" Yet most associates believe that having a clear job description is essential to faithful excellence in ministry. As Mark explains, "A clear job description helps me know what I'm supposed to do and is necessary for fair and helpful evaluation of my work." Evaluation is a key element, but helpful evaluation requires that all parties are clear about the nature of the associate pastor's responsibilities, even when he or she may be asked to do special projects on occasion that go beyond the written job description.

A clear job description provides the foundation for self-differentiation necessary for effectiveness in ministry. As one associate pastor notes, "I can't do everything in this church, so having a job description creates a healthy boundary for me. It keeps me on track, helps me focus my energy, and provides me with a way to say no to some requests that are optional and would be an ineffective use of my time at the church." A clear job description provides a healthy structure for new pastors who need to grow into their professional self-identity. As another associate pastor says, "Without a good job description and an intentional senior pastor, I would have been running all over the place, trying to prove myself in ministry. The job description reminded me that I don't have to do it all; I have colleagues in ministry; and I can turn the lights off and go home."

Until an associate pastor develops a healthy professional identity and sense of call, a good job description provides an external structure and healthy professional limits. In my own experience, the most successful ministries are not done by the clock. Ministry is not a nine-to-five job. Therefore, job descriptions should be flexible in required hours. A strong and healthy senior pastor may have to "put on the brakes," as one associate pastor notes, "when I'm working too hard."

While some weeks, a pastor may work sixty to seventy hours, or even longer in the case of a congregational crisis or a natural disaster, professional wisdom indicates that healthy ministry over the long haul requires rest, retreat, and relationships. When pastors work smart, they can achieve a great deal during a fifty-hour week, with built-in times for prayer, study, and collegial support.

COLLEAGUE GROUPS

Monica affirms the importance of colleague groups for associate ministers. "I need a place I can air my challenges, blow off steam, and seek guidance. You can't do this at the ministerium, because the senior pastor or his best friends may also be in attendance. You need a safe, confidential place for sharing." Sharon has found that an informal support group has enabled her to do creative and healthy ministry. "I meet with a group of four women once a month. We are a sounding board for one another where we can share our challenges in ministry. We discover we're all going through the same things and can provide wisdom and alternatives for one another."

In my work as director of Lancaster Theological Seminary's Wholeness in Ministry program for new pastors, I have created an associate ministers' subgroup, which provides an opportunity for associate pastors to learn from each other, share wisdom, and support each other in their ministries. Each meeting integrates prayer and meditation, scriptural reflection, sharing of joys and concerns, and discussion of a particular topic related to multiple-staff and associate ministry. Over the past five years, participants have commented regularly, "I no longer feel alone; other pastors are experiencing what I'm going through as they try to grow in ministerial effectiveness."

Creative Wisdom for Associate Ministry

The following paragraphs provide spiritual grounding for the best practices that have been discussed throughout this chapter.

SEEING THE LIGHT IN EACH OTHER

The biblical tradition proclaims that humankind, male and female, is created in the image of God. John's Gospel asserts that the light of the world shines in everyone. In this spirit, the following spiritual practice is intended to help you see the divine presence in yourself and in your colleagues in ministry.

Begin by finding a comfortable position and taking a few deep breaths to relax. Close your eyes and breathe gently, experiencing a sense of wholeness and well-being with each breath. Begin experiencing yourself as God's beloved son or daughter, safe and secure in God's loving and protective light.

When you feel sufficiently relaxed, take a moment to begin visualizing your colleague in ministry. Imagine your colleague as a beloved child of God. One way to do this is to imagine him or her surrounded and filled with God's loving and healing light. As you visualize him or her encompassed by God's light, take a moment to say a prayer, asking God to be present in your colleague's life and ministry and asking for a blessing in your relationship together.

Conclude this ten- to fifteen-minute meditation by making a commitment to experience God's light in your colleague, in yourself, and in your relationship. Ask for guidance in bringing out the best in your colleague and your ministry together.

As a footnote to this spiritual practice, let me remind you that while you are always called to pray for your colleagues in ministry, you may also be called to enter into a time of spiritual discernment if your collegial relationship is unhealthy and possibly irreparable. At such moments, the most healing behavior may be to begin the process of moving to another ministerial setting.

LIVING BY THE SERENITY PRAYER

Attributed to theologian Reinhold Niebuhr and central to 12-step programs, the Serenity Prayer can be a source of healing and wholeness for pastors in every season of ministry. In its essence, the Serenity Prayer reminds us that while we are creative decision-makers, our agency as pastors and people always occurs in an environment that is the source of both limitations and possibilities. Associate pastors often have to embody spiritual leadership within a framework of others' visions and decisions and need to make peace with the inherent limitations of their position. As Leigh Ann notes, "Even in a good ministerial situation like my own, there are limits to my autonomy, and I need to fit into the senior pastor's vision. I need to be humble and willing to learn from my colleague." The Serenity Prayer states simply:

> God, grant me the serenity
> to accept the things I cannot change;
> courage to change the things I can;
> and wisdom to know the difference.

By regularly living in accordance with the wisdom of the Serenity Prayer, pastors in every season of life can claim their own voice and agency, their calling to be people of integrity, while recognizing that they live within the limitations of institutional relationships and decisions, personality types of supervisors, accidents, and surprises. Living by the Serenity Prayer helps associate pastors remember that they always have the freedom to choose their attitude toward any circumstance, and in that freedom they can experience a sense of openness to possibility and transformation in any situation.

Pastors can practice the Serenity Prayer by prayerfully reflecting on their current ministerial situation, asking questions such as:

+ What is my responsibility in this situation? Am I a leader or a follower?
+ In what ways can I influence this situation to achieve the well-being of the congregation and the people with whom I minister?
+ If I have no organizational power in this situation, in what ways can I let go of the need for control? How can I support the best interests of the church in this situation?

CHAPTER 12

THE CONTINUING EDUCATION OF NEW PASTORS

And Jesus increased in wisdom and in years, and in divine and human favor.

—LUKE 2:52

WHEN I ASKED DEBBIE, A YOUNG MOTHER THEN IN HER fifth month as associate pastor of an urban congregation in Seattle, Washington, what she was doing for continuing education, her first response surprised me: "Nothing!" But, her next words awakened me to new ways of looking at continuing theological education: "Just out of seminary, with the new baby and new call to ministry, and trying to balance my personal and professional responsibilities with my husband's schedule, my head is bursting with so much data. I don't think I can add anything more, beyond what I'm reading for my monthly sermons."

While I might have been disappointed with the response of this intellectually gifted young pastor, her honesty reminded me that no one pathway to continuing theological education is appropriate to every new pastor or every season of ministry.

Just as people pray in different ways, they also learn in different ways. "The harvest of righteousness" (Phil. 1:11) God seeks for all of us will grow toward fruition through many pathways of spiritual practice and theological education.

Like other seminary professors, I have advised every pastor to have three books of different genres on his or her nightstand—theology or ministry, fiction or poetry, and current events. While that advice is generally sound, such counsel would only add to the guilt that some pastors feel when they compare their experiences in ministry with the ideals they learned in seminary. It might also become an obstacle to their unique ways of learning, appropriate to their particular life circumstances, age, and personality type.

Debbie continued:

> In seminary, my professors implied that the only things worth reading could be found in books, journals, and commentaries. Right now, I barely have time to read a novel as I try to juggle all these new responsibilities. But let me tell you where I am learning new things. I participate in a few online blogs, regularly read commentaries in textweek.com, and download materials that catch my attention on Facebook. I know that I want to study more, but if I focus on the ideal, I'll just feel inadequate.

Debbie added, "I make it a point to listen to NPR when I'm in the car, and hardly ever miss *Speaking of Faith* with Krista Tippett on Sunday afternoons. I find insights in these programs that I wouldn't find in theology texts." Despite her initial confession that she is unable to devote any time to continuing education, in the course of our conversation, Debbie and I both came to realize that at this point in her life, she was intellectually growing, but her primary vehicles of continuing theological education were related to media and social networking. Debbie reminded me that a continuing education diet solely composed of abstract theological texts and biblical commentaries may render a pastor's message irrelevant to the day-to-day experiences of her community.

Aaron, a pastor of a United Methodist Church in suburban Los Angeles, also takes seriously the media as essential to his theological continuing education. A new parent like Debbie, Aaron is interested in ministry with twenty- and thirtysomethings and the insights of the emerging church movement. In describing his own continuing theological education, Aaron says:

> It's a hodgepodge. I go down to Claremont School of Theology monthly to pick up a few books at the library or go to a lecture, but most of my ongoing education comes from two sources—emerging Christianity and young adult ministry websites, and the Sunday New York Times. Checking the New York Times as well as the Los Angeles Times online each day helps me see the big picture of world events and enables me to relate to the concerns of my parishioners, most of whom are highly educated people, working in government, law, consulting, and education. The websites keep me informed about what's going on in ministry today, especially in terms of ways to reach out to my contemporaries.

Aaron also regularly attends workshops and conferences on young adult ministry and emerging Christianity. Aaron affirms, "I always come home from these conferences feeling hopeful and ready to try something new in my ministry." Aaron and Debbie embody in their own practices of continuing education the wisdom that good theology integrates the most imaginative thinking of our time with the great traditions of the past.

Chris, the pastor of a Presbyterian church located between York and Lancaster, Pennsylvania, cites going to movies as important in her ongoing theological education. As we talked over lunch at a restaurant looking out on the Susquehanna River,

Chris recalled that she had recently seen the film *Invictus*, which focuses on Nelson Mandela. This reminded Chris of her congregation's mission trip to South Africa and the seminary cross-cultural experience several years before that had deepened her sense of the spirituality of Mandela and his colleagues. Many preachers such as Chris have noted that movies are significant homiletical points of contact with their parishioners. While we can no longer count on our congregants having a shared awareness of a Shakespeare play, classics in literature, or even the Bible, pastors often find common ground when we discuss the religious dimensions of popular films—for example, *Avatar*, *The Blind Side*, *The Lord of the Rings*, *The Chronicles of Narnia*, *The Matrix*, or the Harry Potter movies. Once upon a time, it was suggested that preachers have the Bible in one hand and the *New York Times* in the other. Today, we might substitute a popular movie or best-selling book, such as *The Shack* or *The Da Vinci Code*.

A visual learner, Andrea, a United Church of Christ pastor in Central Maryland, regularly nurtures her ministerial spirit by going to art galleries and museums.

> I regularly go to art openings and make yearly visits to the Museum of Modern Art in New York and the Smithsonian museums in Washington, DC These are not just getaways, although I spend time with friends, but times for bathing my soul in beauty and creativity. For me, ministry is an artistic enterprise, responding to the challenges of congregants, imagining new programs, and artfully gathering stray thoughts into a weekly sermon. I see myself as an artist of the soul, and artwork helps me stay in touch with my inner creativity.

In the chapter on spirituality, I noted that the counsel to "pray as you can, not as you can't" was liberating for new pastors, especially those who were unable to spend half an hour a day in silent contemplation or to go on regular retreats. This same maxim applies to a new pastor's continuing theological education: Be intentional about your professional growth, but don't let the ideal vision for continuing education prevent you from growing as a pastor dealing with the concrete limitations of day-to-day ministry.

I believe that continuing theological education is essential for good ministry. Pastors are called to be their congregation's rabbis or teachers as well as spiritual guides, pastoral care givers, preachers and liturgists, prophets, and administrators. A commitment to growing in wisdom and in intellectual and personal stature inspires creativity and imagination in every aspect of pastoral ministry. But clearly new pastors can travel many pathways as they seek to grow professionally beyond seminary. Like Debbie and Aaron, most of them want to study more in the practices of ministry, whether preaching, pastoral care, or theology, as well as explore current trends in North American culture and religion. They also recognize that some study is better than none, and that our rabbinical responsibilities as pastors require us to spend time in theological reflection, whether in the library, the pastor's study, online, or while listening to educational radio and television and other media outlets.

Continuing theological education is truly about growing in wisdom and stature. It involves the wisdom born of seeing God's presence unfolding in the everyday details of life as well as the large panorama of history. As God's companion in the creative process, wisdom dances through all things, bringing delight to all creation (Prov. 8). Vital ministry enables us to grow in insight and the ability to see God's movements in all things, including our own ministry. Growing in stature, as my professor Bernard Loomer stated, involves the commitment to embracing the complexity of experience and welcoming novelty, while maintaining your own spiritual and intellectual identity. New ideas, from books, movies, art, or the Internet, enlarge our spirits and enable us to pastor with greater sensitivity and insight.

Going Back to School

A United Church of Christ pastor and Doctor of Ministry student at Lancaster Theological Seminary, Amy confesses that she entered the DMin program because "I realized I was stuck intellectually and professionally, and if I didn't find a way to grow, I would eventually leave ministry." Amy has been energized by new ways of thinking about ministry and the opportunity to be part of a learning community of fellow pastors who are eager to grow in doing ministry.

Trent, a Baptist pastor from Northern California, entered a DMin program in preaching to supplement the courses he took in seminary.

> I believe preaching is essential to personal and congregational transformation. When I left seminary and took my first call, I realized that I still had a lot to learn in order to be a truly effective preacher. At first, I went to a variety of workshops, including the Festival of Preaching. But I wanted more depth. I wanted to embody my theology of preaching and recognition of the power of the Word to transform lives. The only way I felt I could do that was to go back to school. Good preaching is not optional for me, and going back to school forced me to grow in my preaching.

Both Trent and Amy report that their congregations have greatly appreciated their ongoing commitment to continuing education and see the results in their growth as pastors.

A second-career Presbyterian pastor, Chris acknowledges her continual growth as a theologian. As an intuitive and imagistic person, Chris seeks to bring a creative approach to Scripture in contrast to an analytic and abstract one. Chris confesses, "At first, I had trouble speaking for God yet I have to preach about God!" While Chris will always remain appropriately humble as a preacher and pastor, she has sought to be a lifelong learner. Currently, she is taking a preaching course at the Eastern Mennonite University extension program. To grow in her worship planning and congregational leadership, she also participated in Lancaster Theological Seminary's "Springs of Living Water Seminar for New Pastors," led by Church of the Brethren pastor David Young,[1] as well as the seminary's "Enlivening Worship and Music in the Small Church" program.[2] Like many other new pastors, Chris regularly enrolls in short-term summer enrichment courses, such as those offered through Lancaster Theological Seminary's Summer Academy.[3]

Learning Communities

Many new pastors say that the best venues for continuing theological and professional education are to be found in group settings. Monica, a United Church of Christ solo pastor of a congregation near State College, Pennsylvania, notes that her participation in Lancaster Theological Seminary's Wholeness in Ministry program for new pastors has been essential for her ongoing professional growth. Monica affirms that she "has learned a great deal from colleagues who are in the same situation as I am, beginning their ministries, discerning whether to stay where they are, or facing the challenges of congregational life."

Wholeness in Ministry colleague groups meet for a full day three to four times a year. In addition, two to three plenary programs, bringing together all of the colleague groups, are sponsored throughout the year. Each colleague group integrates prayer and contemplation, sharing joys and challenges in ministry and exploring a specific theme for group theological and professional reflection. Meetings focus on themes such as preaching and worship, personal boundaries, spiritual discernment, dealing with resistance, preaching through the seasons of the Christian year, authority, and creative use of time.

Monica has also found ongoing growth through sponsoring a lectionary reading group in her church. Each week, Monica meets with five to eight congregants for a dialogue on the lectionary readings for the upcoming week. Monica asserts that the group "feeds me in an amazing way. It helps me focus and get to know them better. I bring the liberal perspective to the gatherings, but have also learned a good deal about where they're coming from theologically and culturally. I really get to know them as people, and this helps me be a better preacher and pastor." Monica has begun to supplement her group theological education with online courses offered from her alma mater, Andover Newton Theological School.[4] "I live over two hours from a seminary, so it's difficult to take a class locally. I looked at online options, and I found the course 'Getting and Keeping Volunteers' helpful as I begin my new congregational call. Taking the course from Andover Newton also helped me feel more connected with my alma mater."

Stephen, a United Methodist pastor in rural Virginia, notes the value of being part of an online continuing education program: "The online discussions among class members have given me a larger perspective on my work and also enabled me to get to know a few new friends with whom I now correspond on the Internet. We share one another's ministerial challenges as small town pastors and explore new ideas with one another."

Joanne, a United Church of Christ pastor serving in the Allentown, Pennsylvania, area, gathers regularly with a handful of pastors for a lectionary study. "The group began as a study group but has evolved into a mutual support group. We share our insights on the upcoming readings, but we also share new ideas for ministry and places where we are feeling frustrated with our congregations." Like the Lancaster Theological Seminary's Wholeness in Ministry colleague group in which Joanne participated for four years, this informal group provides the opportunity for safe sharing and exploring alternative ways to look at ministerial leadership as well as the lectionary readings.

Mark, a United Church of Christ pastor in Chambersburg, Pennsylvania, who is also a member of the Lancaster Theological Seminary new pastors' program, regularly participates in a local ecumenical support and accountability group. Mark explains, "The three of us meet as professional colleagues to support and encourage one another in ministry. We're currently reading *The Spiritual Leader's Guide to Self-Care* as the focus on our conversations."[5]

It takes a village of clergy colleagues and lay companions to nurture a new pastor. Our ongoing growth in ministerial identity and professionalism results from the creative interplay of prayerful contemplation, group support, and participation in learning opportunities offered by judicatories and seminaries.

The Pastor as Reader

One of my favorite images of pastoral life is found in the film *A River Runs Through It*, based on Norman Maclean's short story about the relationship between two brothers, sons of a Presbyterian pastor. In the film, Rev. Maclean has two passions, reflecting the traditional affirmation that God has given us two books—the book of Scripture and the book of nature. Rev. Maclean rejoices in the book of nature through his passion for fly-fishing. But he also rejoices in God's revealed words through the Scriptures and theological commentaries. His office is littered with open books—not only Bibles in English, Greek, and Hebrew but also theological texts and poetry.

According to tradition, the book and the scholar's robe reflected the pastor's rabbinical vocation. We are the theologians of our congregations and ministers of Word who serve as the primary teachers of our congregations, even if we happen to have seminary and religion professions among our regular worshipers. We are called to grow as creative interpreters of divine wisdom through our commitment to integrate the wisdom of Scripture with the best contemporary thinking. As John Wesley and others noted, God's wisdom is revealed in the dynamic interplay of Scripture, reason, experience, and tradition, and the pastor as congregational theologian and rabbi had better take all of these seriously. I would add that God is revealed in culture as well, and this challenges pastors to take seriously the insights of literature, psychology, and science as well as various forms of media. While reading is not a popular pastime for all pastors, many have found a steady diet of solid theological reading and literature essential to their growth in ministerial leadership.

In addition to participating in a local colleague group and Lancaster Seminary's Wholeness in Ministry program for new pastors, Mark reads widely, books that reflect his interests as well as novels, theological texts, and congregational leadership books. "Right, now," Mark reported, "I'm reading Cornel West's memoir, *Brother West: Living and Loving Out Loud.*"[6] In that same spirit, Chris tries to read selected books from the *New York Times* best sellers in fiction. In addition to keeping up with books in theology and congregational life, Chris finds that fiction feeds her imagination and enables her to be a more insightful preacher and pastor. In the spirit of Jesus's parables, Mark, Chris, and many other new pastors have discovered that religious insight is often shared more creatively through images and poetry than catechetical or doctrinal exposition.

Creative Wisdom for Theological Education

When I accepted my first ministerial call as Protestant chaplain at Georgetown University, I immediately realized how much I didn't know about ministry. With most of my graduate training in theology and philosophy of religion, I knew that I needed to scramble to gain both confidence and expertise in many of the arts of ministry. Therefore, I embarked on a journey of professional growth through involvement in seminars and workshops, study, and conversations with peers and experienced pastors. I also was—and still am—fortunate to be married to Kate Epperly, who had ministerial experience in some of the areas in which I felt deficient. I also followed my intellectual and spiritual passions—and still continue to follow my passion and energy—for exploring the frontiers of theology and pastoral ministry. In the early 1980s, as I began my seventeen-year journey as a university chaplain, I discovered that I had a strong interest in healing and wholeness, interfaith dialogue, and practical theology. This led me to attend lectures at the Georgetown University School of Medicine, learn the energy healing technique of reiki healing touch, study liturgical healing and healing prayer, and begin spiritual formation groups for medical students and staff. I also involved myself in interfaith dialogue groups with my colleagues in the university chaplaincy. I took courses offered by the counseling center on depression, grief, and suicide prevention and eventually initiated a grief support group for students, staff, and faculty at the university.

I believe that the key to effective ongoing theological and ministerial education is integrating self-awareness and passion. In this spirit, I invite you to take some time to consider the following questions related to your current ministerial practices:

+ About which arts of ministry—for example, counseling, teaching, preaching, Scripture, administration, social justice, evangelism, spiritual direction—do I feel most deficient or anxious?
+ What new skills in ministry do I need to acquire, or what do I need to improve, in order to be a more effective leader in my current congregation?
+ What intellectual or theological horizons lure me forward?

Let your answers to these questions guide you toward appropriate and accessible learning opportunities.

Second, consider the ways you learn best. Discovering your unique learning style will enable you to learn in a way more congruent with your gifts. It may also challenge you to explore other learning styles, or what have been called *multiple intelligences*. If certain learning styles are particularly challenging for you, self-awareness may help you respond creatively in order to find other more effective avenues for your own learning.

Third, reflect on your current passions for ongoing professional and theological growth. For example, my passion for healing led me to explore both complementary medicine and Christian healing techniques. Over the years, I have written a number of books, and I regularly lead retreats and teach classes, on Christian healing. Living out this passion has energized my ministry, deepened my spiritual life, and enabled me to be a healing partner with individuals and families facing chronic or critical health issues.

As you reflect on your personal passions for effective ministry and spiritual leadership, you may choose to consider prayerfully the following questions:

+   Where do I feel a deep passion that is currently untapped in my ministry? How might I creatively respond to that passion for my own and my congregation's spiritual growth?
+   Where do I feel God calling me as a next step in spiritual leadership? How might I most creatively address God's call?

Congregational leadership is a holy adventure lived in companionship with an adventurous God, who truly wants us to grow in wisdom and stature in our ministries. Faithful excellence in ministry emerges and is nurtured in the ongoing quest to grow in professional skill, practical application, theological insight, and spiritual depth.

Concluding Blessing: Staying in the Spirit

Very truly, I tell you, the one who believes in me will also do
the works that I do and, in fact, will do greater works than
these, because I am going to the Father.

—JOHN 14:12

I can do all things through [God] who strengthens me. . . .
And my God will fully satisfy every need of yours according
to his riches in glory in Christ Jesus.

—PHILIPPIANS 4:13, 19

To say that these are challenging times for pastors is to state
the obvious. Anxiety abounds in congregations and denominations, and it is easy to succumb to fear and scarcity thinking,
even though God promises abundant life. More than one new
pastor has noted, "I have no idea where the church is going today and what the future will be. I'm uncertain if I will be working full time in ministry five years from now, given the reality of
the churches in our area."

While knowing that life in the first-century church was also
uncertain and the future for Christian communities was tenuous
at best is little comfort for today's pastors, healthy and effective
pastors need to find ways to stay with God's Spirit as they lead
congregations in a rapidly changing and uncertain time. There
are no best practices that work for everyone in ministry, but
there are many helpful ministerial practices—grounded in the
dynamic interplay of Scripture, theological education, practical
wisdom, self-care, and healthy relatedness—that can provide a
sense of wholeness and peace for pastors, even in anxious times.

This book began with the affirmation that "the one who
began a good work among you will bring it to completion by
the day of Jesus Christ . . . the harvest of righteousness" (Phil.
1:6, 11). This is the promise that undergirds both ministry and
congregational life, evident in the following ministerial and
congregational affirmations:

+   God is at our work in our lives, the church, and the world.
+   God seeks our wholeness and fulfillment.
+   God is present in the small and large details of our lives.
+   God desires that I live out faithful excellence in my vocation as pastor.
+   God will have the final word, and it is abundant fruitfulness.

Staying with the Spirit that inspired our first steps in ministry involves responding faithfully to God's graceful presence in our lives. Nurtured by God's presence in our lives, we can respond as pastors with openness and fidelity. We practice opening ourselves to God's Spirit through commitment to prayer, meditation, professional growth, health and wellness, and nurturing relationships. God still has great things in store for us and the church, and calls us forward to a holy adventure with God as our guide, companion, advocate, and support.

May you experience God's creative wisdom and dynamic presence as you go forth as God's companion in ministry! Amen.

NOTES

Introduction: Starting with Spirit

1.   For more on the Lancaster Theological Seminary programs for pastors as well as ministerial wholeness at every stage of ministry, see Bruce G. Epperly and Katherine Gould Epperly, *Four Seasons of Ministry: Gathering a Harvest of Righteousness* (Herndon, VA: Alban Institute, 2008).

2.   Lillian Daniel and Martin B. Copenhaver, *This Odd and Wondrous Calling: The Public and Private Lives of Two Ministers* (Grand Rapids: Wm. B. Eerdmanns, 2009), 2.

3.   Barbara Brown Taylor, *Leaving Church: A Memoir of Faith* (New York: HarperSanFrancisco, 2006), 75, 98–99.

4.   Katherine Gould Epperly and I have explored the intersection of theology and spirituality in healthy and effective ministry in our trilogy: *Feed the Fire! Avoiding Clergy Burnout* (Cleveland: Pilgrim Press, 2008); *Four Seasons of Ministry: Gathering a Harvest of Righteousness* (Herndon, VA: Alban Institute, 2008); *Tending to the Holy: The Practice of the Presence of God in Ministry* (Herndon: VA: Alban Institute, 2009).

5.   Craig Dykstra, "The Pastoral Imagination," *Initiatives in Religion* 9, no. 1 (Spring 2001), 2–3, 15.

Chapter 1: Opening the Door

1.   Richard Lischer, *Open Secrets: A Memoir of Faith and Discovery* (New York: Broadway Books, 2002), 8–9.

2.   Reinhold Niebuhr, *Leaves from the Notebook of a Tamed Cynic* (New York: Meridian Books, 1959), 9

3.   Ibid., 11.

4.   Lischer, *Open Secrets*, 49.

5.   Ibid., 49.

6.   Ibid., 56.

7.   For more on programs for new pastors sponsored by Lancaster Theological Seminary and other seminary and judicatory agencies, see Bruce G. Epperly and Katherine Gould Epperly, *The Four Seasons of Ministry: Gathering a Harvest of Righteousness* (Herndon, VA: Alban Institute, 2008).

CHAPTER 2: WHAT I DIDN'T LEARN IN SEMINARY, AND WHAT SEMINARIES CAN LEARN FROM NEW PASTORS

1.   Katherine Gould Epperly and I deal with the spirituality of administration in *Tending to the Holy: The Practice of the Presence of God in Ministry*, (Herndon: VA: Alban Institute, 2009), 119–58.

2.   Bruce Epperly and Daryl Hollinger, *From a Mustard Seed: Enlivening Worship and Music in the Small Church* (Herndon, VA: Alban Institute, 2010).

3.   For one path to creative and spiritually grounded preaching, see Epperly and Epperly, *Tending to the Holy*, 19–60. I regularly write lectionary commentaries for Process and Faith (www.processandfaith.org/lectionary).

4.   For more on these issues see Bruce G. Epperly and Katherine Gould Epperly, *Four Seasons of Ministry: Gathering a Harvest of Righteousness* (Herndon, VA: Alban Institute, 2008); and *Feed the Fire! Avoiding Clergy Burnout* (Cleveland: Pilgrim Press, 2008).

CHAPTER 3: AUTHORITY AND RELATIONSHIP IN THE CHURCH

1.   For more on this vision of God, see Bruce Epperly, *Holy Adventure: 41 Days of Audacious Living* (Nashville: Upper Room, 2008).

2.   For more on congregational systems theory, see Edwin Friedman, *Generation to Generation: Family Process in Church and Synagogue* (New York: Guilford Press, 1985); and Peter L. Steinke, *Congregational Leadership in Anxious Times: Being Calm and Courageous No Matter What* (Herndon, VA: Alban Institute, 2006).

3.   Celia Hahn, *Growing in Authority, Relinquishing Control: A New Approach to Faithful Leadership* (Herndon, VA: Alban Institute, 1994).

4.   Jackson Carroll, *As One with Authority* (Louisville: Westminster John Knox, 1991), 98.

5.   For more on creative responses to resistance, see Bruce G. Epperly and Katherine Gould Epperly, *Feed the Fire! Avoiding Clergy Burnout*

(Cleveland: Pilgrim Press, 2008); and *Tending to the Holy: The Practice of the Presence of God in Ministry* (Herndon, VA: Alban Institute, 2009); and William Chris Hobgood, *Welcoming Resistance: A Path to Faithful Ministry* (Herndon, VA: Alban Institute, 2002).

6. *The Book of Common Prayer* (New York: Oxford University Press, 1990), 531.

7. *Book of Worship of the United Church of Christ* (New York: United Church of Christ Office for Church Life and Leadership, 1986), 407–8.

8. Carroll, *As One with Authority*, 14.

9. Bernard Loomer, "Two Conceptions of Power," *Process Studies* 6:1 (Spring 1976): 5–32.

10. Steinke, *Congregational Leadership in Anxious Times*, xi.

11. Ibid., 134.

CHAPTER 4: WHEN THE HONEYMOON'S OVER, IF THERE EVER WAS ONE

1. Diana Butler Bass, *Christianity for the Rest of Us: How the Neighborhood Church Is Transforming the Faith* (New York: Harper One, 2007); Dorothy Bass, *Practicing Our Faith: A Way of Life for a Searching People* (San Francisco: Jossey-Bass, 2010); and Miroslav Wolf and Dorothy C. Bass, eds., *Practicing Theology: Beliefs and Practices in the Christian Life* (Grand Rapids: Eerdmans, 2001).

2. For more on responding creatively to the challenges of resistance, see William Chris Hobgood, *Welcoming Resistance: A Path to Faithful Ministry* (Herndon, VA: Alban Institute, 2001).

3. See Bruce G. Epperly and Katherine Gould Epperly, *Tending to the Holy: The Practice of the Presence of God in Ministry* (Herndon, VA: Alban Institute, 2009).

CHAPTER 5: BOUNDARIES THAT HEAL PASTORS AND CONGREGATIONS

1. Nina McIntosh, *The Educated Heart: Professional Boundaries for Massage Therapists, Bodyworkers, and Movement Teachers* (Philadelphia: Lippencott, Williams, and Wilkins, 2005), 5.

CHAPTER 6: THE INNOVATIVE PASTOR

1. William Chris Hobgood, *Welcoming Resistance: A Path to Faithful Ministry* (Herndon, VA: Alban Institute, 2002).

2.   Jan Karon, *At Home in Mitford* (New York: Penguin Books, 1996), the first of nine Mitford books.

3.   Bruce Epperly and Katherine Gould Epperly, *Four Seasons of Ministry: Gathering a Harvest of Righteousness* (Herndon, VA: Alban Institute, 2008), 3.

4.   Ibid., 25–26.

Chapter 7: Death Never Takes a Holiday
for Pastors and Congregations

1.   Nelle Morton, *The Journey Is Home* (Boston: Beacon Press Books, 1985), 205.

Chapter 8: The Spiritual Lives of
Spiritual Leaders

1.   Rueben Job, *Three Simple Rules: The Wesleyan Way of Living* (Nashville: Abingdon, 2007).

2.   Bruce G. Epperly and Katherine Gould Epperly, *Reiki Healing Touch and the Way of Jesus* (Kelowna, BC: Northstone, 2006).

3.   Bruce G. Epperly and Katherine Gould Epperly, *Tending to the Holy: The Practice of the Presence of God in Ministry* (Herndon: VA: Alban Institute, 2009), 16–18.

Chapter 12: The Continuing Education
of New Pastors

1.   David S. Young, *Streams of Living Water: Christ-Centered Church Renewal* (Scottdale, PA: Herald Press, 2008).

2.   For more on this program, see Bruce G. Epperly and Daryl Hollinger, *From a Mustard Seed: Enlivening Worship and Music in the Small Church* (Herndon, VA: Alban Institute, 2010).

3.   For more on Lancaster Theological Seminary's continuing education programs for pastors, please consult www.lancasterseminary.edu or www.livingtheadventure.org.

4.   For more on Andover Newton Theological School's online program, see www.ants.edu/learn.

5.   Rochelle Melander and Harold Eppley, *The Spiritual Leader's Guide to Self-Care* (Herndon, VA: Alban, 2002).

6.   Cornel West and David Ritz, *Brother West: Living and Loving Out Loud* (New York: Smiley Books, 2009).